Praise for *Lose Well*

"If anyone can get you to giv... ...Chris Gethard, the king of someh...

—Judd Apatow, comedian

"This is funny, sure, but it's very much more. Chris speaks inspirational life truths to the outsider in all of us. A pithy road map of the antiestablishment path by which one can succeed in comedy and life. Gethard gets it."

—Nick Offerman, actor, comedian, and author of the *New York Times* bestselling *Paddle Your Own Canoe*

"I was on the altar at Chris Gethard's wedding when he was waiting a really long time for his bride to show up. Like, so long. I figured, based on his past life experiences, that it wasn't going to end well. Anyway, that's what this book is like."

—Mike Birbiglia, comedian, actor, and author of the *New York Times* bestselling *Sleepwalk with Me—and Other Painfully True Stories*

". . . Gethard's writing style is effortless and enjoyable, and his beliefs are compassionate and encouraging. Fans will be thrilled to dive deeper into his life and work, and anyone else stuck in a rut will find permission to go out and try—and fail—as often and as well as possible."

—*Publishers Weekly*

"Chris Gethard's *Lose Well* will change the way you think about failure. It's funny, heartfelt, and full of advice that every creative person needs to hear."

—Hello Giggles

". . . the sort of vulnerable, honest, and spoken-from-experience material that's earned him such a strong online following . . . and qualifies him to write a book like *Lose Well*."

—The A.V. Club

LOSE WELL

FALSE STARTS, BEAUTIFUL DISASTERS, PUBLIC HUMILIATIONS, AND OTHER SECRETS TO SUCCESS

CHRIS GETHARD

HarperOne

An Imprint of HarperCollinsPublishers

To my father.
Early in life you taught me
the value of hard work. Later you showed me
the importance of enjoying the life you work hard for.
While we've never said it out loud to each other,
I want you to know that I love you.

HarperOne

LOSE WELL. Copyright © 2018 by Chris Gethard. All rights reserved. Printed in the United States of America. No part of this book may be used or reproduced in any manner whatsoever without written permission except in the case of brief quotations embodied in critical articles and reviews. For information, address HarperCollins Publishers, 195 Broadway, New York, NY 10007.

HarperCollins books may be purchased for educational, business, or sales promotional use. For information, please email the Special Markets Department at SPsales@harpercollins.com.

FIRST HARPERCOLLINS PAPERBACK EDITION PUBLISHED IN 2019

Designed by Ad Librum

Library of Congress Cataloging-in-Publication Data is available upon request.

ISBN 978-0-06-269142-2

19 20 21 22 23   LSC   10 9 8 7 6 5 4 3 2 1

CONTENTS

Preface v

Introduction 1

Lose Well 19

You Are the Chaos 33

But No One I Know Does This Stuff 41

Bye Bye Birdie 47

Why This? Why Here? Why Now? 59

Pfizer Winter 63

When Should I Quit? 75

The Falcon 77

Stop Apologizing 87

Punk 97

Never Let Them See the Scales 109

No Need for Rock Bottom 115

"It's Too Late" 119

Weird N.J. 125

"No One Will Get It" 141

Dusty Bunter: True Scum 147

Bitterness Is the Enemy 159

Greggulation 161

Public Access 169

Red Light Rules 197

The Unusual Things 207

Funny Plus 209

Always Be Terrified 219

Pushing Through Blocks 225

The Current State of Things 229

Acknowledgments 241

PREFACE

Hello! Welcome to the paperback!

Congratulations on waiting out the initial wave of curiosity you had regarding this book. You've saved yourself a sweet ten dollars. Let's be honest, there are benefits and drawbacks. This version looks less distinguished on your bookshelf. It isn't as usable as a coaster. You can't brandish it to smash a rich person's window when the inevitable class war erupts. But on the plus side, it doesn't weigh as much. That's better for your back, and the smaller trim size makes it easier to carry in a bag, which is nice because it allows you to read incrementally in public and not make eye contact with other people.

For the paperback edition, I wanted to include a few things that have been on my mind since the book's initial publication. So not only did you spend *less* money, you get slightly *more* words. That's smart consumer-ship, and I applaud your ability to game the capitalist system. Paying less to get more is one of the great feelings in this world, ranking at the exact midpoint between unsubscribing from an email list you never signed up for and orgasm. Kudos to you, my friend.

A lot has changed in my life over the past year. Because a particularly big professional development will color how you read one of the book's main topics, I want to address that. Another life change reframes the purpose of my existence, so I imagine that deserves a cursory mention as well.

You're going to read a bunch of stories in the coming pages. Some are funny. Some are philosophical. Some give concrete advice. Spoiler alert! They all lead to me achieving an unlikely dream: hosting my own talk show on cable television. Just after the hardcover went on sale, however, that show got canceled. Kaput. That dream died. My weird variety show wasn't built to last. Mainstream viewers didn't love my strange alternative comedy bits. An episode we did with Will Ferrell got so bizarre that online conspiracy theorists are now convinced I'm part of Pizzagate. (Google it: they swear I'm a key cog in an underground satanic Hollywood cult.) At the end of the day, the network's regular audience didn't want to watch me get trapped in a cage while one hundred pounds of human hair dropped on me. They much preferred reruns of a show featuring four affable friends from Staten Island pranking unsuspecting patrons in a mall food court. Honestly? I get it.

All this is to say, you're now holding in your hands a bunch of chapters that detail how *YOU TOO* might be able to live your dream until it falls on its face and departs this world. Not with a bang, but with a whimper. Mine is not as happy an ending as it once was.

And I think that's great. It's a test of the very theories I lay out in this book, and I'm happy to report that the past year has only strengthened my belief in the healing and restorative power of failing. After my show was canceled, I didn't get sad—not even for one day. Like I say in the book, failure is your friend, and losing well is just your next first step on the way to potential happiness. Even after my most recent flameout—which unfolded live on national television at the same time every week—I believe this sentiment is truer than ever, and as I start to develop new projects, I feel its message even more strongly in my bones.

It's also strengthened my hope that my failure may be your gain. If there's one reason I'm proud that this book exists, it's the hope that by demystifying my own relationship with some very public failures, you might be able to avoid the pitfalls I've either fallen into or jumped headfirst into. I genuinely want you to get where you want to go with fewer headaches and less bullshit. I hope I can help.

I'm not saying you need to fail on national television to get there. I just believe my own *very* public failures might help. I'd love for these thoughts, anecdotes, and insights to feel useful—and just as importantly, honest—to you. I'm not trying to sell you on theoretical fluff. All of my lessons have been lived, and I bet your versions of these livable lessons are within reach. If this book helps expose them, I'd feel like it's been worth it.

This leads me to something I also want to address, something I didn't include in the hardcover: why I was motivated to write this book in the first place.

There were a few factors. First, I was flattered to be approached about trying my hand at it and must admit that I enjoy paying my rent through creative endeavors. Writing a book is a hard thing to do, and a cool thing to do, and when someone challenges you to do it *and* says they'll pay you for your efforts, I think you should dive right in. But I promise you, money was not the motivating factor. If anything, I was ultra-aware of making sure it wasn't. Self-help is not something I'm an authority on, and I felt a lot of responsibility going there.

I get why it makes sense for me to try my hand at this. I've made some projects in the past that struck an emotional chord with people. My HBO special *Career Suicide* talked in depth about my mental illness. My podcast *Beautiful Stories from Anonymous People* features conversations with anonymous callers about topics that range from silly to as serious as it gets, and I always try to provide a judgment-free place for people to get their stories on record. Because of that, I see how I sit on a strange point of the Venn diagram where it does make sense for me, a comedian with a worthless state school degree in American studies, to try my hand at self-help.

But that needs to be born out of a genuine desire to help. In my opinion, when self-help is a moneymaking scheme it can get gross fast. I don't want to sell you snake oil. I don't want to be a self-styled guru. There's a slippery slope with this self-help stuff, and the last thing I'd want is to become the next Gwyneth Paltrow. It starts with me detailing how the shitty stand-up comedy gigs I've worked made me a better artist and human, then the next thing you know it's six months later and I'm trying to sell you a polished stone you can rub on your genitals in order to have more vibrant skin. No thanks.

Before writing this book, I took a deep breath and thought about if it was right and responsible for me to work in this space. Two conversations helped justify my attempt and lit a bright fire in my guts.

As I pondered who would get something out of this book, my thoughts kept returning to a conversation I had with an old friend. We went to high school together and, once in a blue moon, still kept in touch. One night, she sent me a message asking if we could get dinner. She told me she wanted to pick my brain about some stuff.

At an old-school pizzeria in Manhattan, my friend told me that she'd always wanted to give comedy a try and wanted to know how I'd approached it. This is a conversation all comedians learn to avoid. After pretty much every gig, you get some fresh-faced kid who wants you to validate their dreams. It's nice, but also a little bit frustrating, because the answer is, generally, "You gotta just go out and do it."

But my friend's situation was different. She was a single mom. She wasn't someone who could "just go out and do it." Her life circumstances didn't exactly lend themselves to that kind of hopeful recklessness.

Until she asked me to consider my career—literally how I had made it happen—I hadn't thought much about the relative advantages I had pursuing it: I'm a white guy, I'm married to a lady, I have parents who aren't going to let me starve.

Not everyone has such a clear path. My initial inspiration became this: "Maybe if I write down every motivating moment or philosophy that's helped me along the way I can expose the gears of the machine for my friend." Since then, I've worked hard to expand that philosophy for anyone who's looking for the motivation to try.

Writing this book, I often thought of a talk I gave at a public library in a rough section of Elizabeth, New Jersey. A friend of mine worked there and she told me that a lot of the kids in her after-school program were the artsy kids around town. They hung out in the library because that's where they felt okay about being the weird ones. She thought maybe hearing from another weird kid from North Jersey who found some success in the arts would inspire them.

That speech was . . . not good. I've never missed the mark harder. I've never felt more tone deaf, more obtuse. I tried to give a rousing speech about how I chased my dreams by setting aside an emergency bank account, which you'll read about later. They looked at me like I had two heads. The idea that you could set any money aside was not part of their reality. They didn't have disposable income. Their existence was much more day-to-day than mine has ever had to be. Framing my speech around how I used my surplus income was, simply put, not cool.

I hope some of these kids find this book, and I hope that there are sections that speak more to who they are and where they're at. If any of them—or any of the kids cut from a similar cloth in cities all across America—find even a shred of useful advice in the following chapters, I will be thrilled to no end. I hope I've translated the lessons I've learned into ones anyone can put to use in their own lives regardless of their background or circumstance. In its best moments, I hope that this book can specifically help those who most feel that chasing their dreams is an uphill climb.

I think of many of the callers I've spoken to on *Beautiful/Anonymous*. The last three years of phone calls have allowed me to speak to a diverse array of people, but many of them share a common feeling: that they are not listened to. I think of how many callers have told me about having parents who messed up their lives, or partners who messed with their heads, or bosses who messed with their confidence.

I hope all of them can use some of the dumb lessons I've accrued along the way to backdoor their way into some momentum. It would mean the world to me.

To be perfectly honest, despite my relative success in entertainment, I never felt like I was "of" the industry. I view my experience navigating that world less as someone trying to fit into it and more like a hacker, or an old-school phone phreak: someone who enters the system to see how its guts work, to figure out how it can be manipulated.

Don't get me wrong: I cut no corners. I worked my ass off. I tried to stand out in the New York comedy scene, which is full of people funnier than me. (And a million other white dudes with glasses.) I faced down self-doubt and depression along the way. I dealt with dishonest people, soul-sucking gigs, and many other obstacles you'll soon read about. Undoubtedly, you face your own obstacles. Our paths might not be the same, but maybe some of the fight we find to deal with those obstacles are. If showing you my battle scars helps you avoid accruing some of your own, I'd be thrilled.

Consider this book my field report of a life spent trying to game the various systems in front of me. I hope some others can game it easier and quicker, with a greater yield in results, via the experiences I recount in this cheap, light paperback book.

Oh! Before I forget: I mentioned that I had a life-changing development that redefined my very existence. Can't bring that up and never address it again.

Less than a year after this book was released and my television show was canceled, my wife gave birth to our first child. As I write this, he's sleeping in a weird, donut-shaped pillow on the floor in front of me. He is perfect. He's a cool little dude.

While I'm tempted to write something about how his birth coming in the wake of a massive speed bump in my career feels providential, that's not fair to him. He doesn't need to serve as some karmic symbol. It would be about my path, not his, and I won't put that on him. He doesn't owe me anything. All he has to do is be himself.

That said, I'm very happy he exists, and I'm excited to know that he might check out this book someday. When he does, I hope I'm still subscribing to and living by the ethics I discuss in the following pages. If I set any example for my son as he grows up, I hope it's that I prioritize happiness over money, and fulfillment over fame. Those are codes of honor I'd love to maintain, for both of our sakes.

I thank you, dear reader, for the opportunity to remind myself of the ethics that have kept my head above water. I genuinely hope that they may help you do the same.

Sincerely, and good luck,
Chris Gethard

INTRODUCTION

The best advice I ever received came from my shrink, which is good since I pay her a lot of money.

By 2007 I'd been doing comedy for seven years, which felt like *forever*. Now I'm seventeen years in and feel like I'm still just getting started. Seven years of hard work is nothing. I didn't know that then. I thought I was striking out, that I'd missed my chance. I was twenty-six years old and I was over the hill.

It sounds ridiculous now, but back then those feelings were very, very real. Stress wasn't a faraway concern. It was a minute-by-minute reality. I couldn't sleep. I couldn't think straight. I couldn't make decisions. My anxiety was way beyond normal. At the start of any idea, any venture of any kind, I was paralyzed with fear.

One Friday night I arrived at the UCB Theatre, where I was scheduled to perform with the Stepfathers, an esteemed improv group I'd helped found years earlier. We were all sitting backstage getting ready to go on, just like every week. Joking around. Then the house manager told us it was showtime and everyone stood up. But I . . . *couldn't*. I don't know how to explain it except to say that my body refused to stand up. Fear stabbed me in the gut, twisting the knife around until the tears came. My teammates asked me what was wrong. I shrugged. No words came. I couldn't explain. Nothing was wrong, but everything was wrong.

They went onstage. What else could they do? I sat in the back, feeling all the bad feelings I'd felt prior to now with the added guilt that I'd let down my friends. Staff from the theater asked me questions I couldn't answer. I couldn't speak. The only thing I could do was make eye contact through a torrent of tears, hoping it was enough that they'd read in my eyes the words *I DON'T KNOW WHAT'S GOING ON BUT IT'S BAD.*

I felt broken.

Eventually, people shuffled me off to a back room. Someone put my coat over my shoulders. I heard whispers on the other side of the door as everyone debated what they should do. I heard the word *hospital,* which struck me as a good idea. Then someone said, "I have his brother's number," and the next thing I knew my friend Justin snuck me out the back door and walked me to his place a few blocks away, where I sat motionless, in complete silence until my brother showed up. On zero notice, he had driven up from Philly. I don't remember what we did. I think he took me back to my place. All I know for sure was that he saved me.

That was the final breaking point at the end of a long line of incidents that led me back into the care of a psychiatric professional, the one who would soon give me the best advice I ever received, which again, I'm psyched about because I paid a pretty penny for it.

At the start of one session, my therapist told me, "Give yourself no other option."

It came out of nowhere.

"What's that mean?" I asked.

"You seem to think the thing that's killing you is the potential for failure. It's not. It's that you don't know. You think you can be a comedian, a writer, an actor. You think you have what it takes. But you're not sure. That's the issue here. You'll be fine if it turns out you're a failure. It's living like this, where you're half in, half out, not sure. That's what's causing all this."

"Okay . . ."

"So give yourself no other option. If you think this is something you can really do, go do it. Don't accept money for anything that's not the things you want to do. No more teaching classes. No more freelance magazine writing. You take money for getting onstage, for writing comedy, for acting. That's it. No other option."

"That's a horrible idea."

"Why?"

"I have rent to pay. And bills and stuff."

"Yeah, I know."

"But . . . you don't seem to . . . I pay my rent with the teaching and magazine stuff."

"Yeah, stop that."

"But—"

"Look, shit or get off the pot. Stop taking money for all those things today. And go see if you can get money for the other stuff. And if you can, great, you were right. A lot of this will go away. And if you can't, you'll know that. Not everybody has what it takes. I think you could make it if you really go for it. But you might not. Trust me, you'll like knowing you fell on your face and can move on, versus this floating-in-the-middle-ground nonsense."

And so I did. I gave myself no other option. I set aside $2,000 as my "break glass in case of emergency" money. I lived off the rest of my savings and whatever else I could scratch together from gigs, just enough to pay my rent and bills and eat for a month. At the very least, if I ever had to scramble and find a nine-to-five, I always knew I had that two grand to pay my rent and hold me over until

I did. I decided that when that $2,000 was all I had left, I would officially pronounce my dream over. At that point, I would have to move on.

The next year was terrifying. I watched my savings account tick away like a doomsday clock. Every once in a while I'd land an unexpected job that added a few more seconds back to the clock. These jobs were always weird.

I once booked a stand-up gig at a festival. Sounds cool, right? Festival dates are usually fun. You get to see bands, and people walk around naked, and because the comedy tent is one of the only air-conditioned places at a festival it's always full and the crowds are always grateful to be there.

This was not one of those festival gigs. I hosted a side stage for a car company. This side stage was *not* advertised in any of the festival literature, so no one knew it existed.

My job was to do crowd work in between the bands to ensure fans stuck around throughout the day. I'm guessing the car company's idea was that, somehow, these drug-addled millennials would say to themselves, *You know what? I came here for the music, but I think at this point I'll purchase an automobile.*

Occasionally a handful of people would stick around and watch in confusion as I took the stage and told jokes, only to wander away when they realized the next band wasn't coming on any time soon. The first time the crowd bottomed out I walked offstage. The guy who booked me ran up in a panic.

"What are you doing? Get back out there!"

"But . . . there's no one there."

"But they'll come. That's the whole point! If you're doing stuff, they'll stop; they'll come!"

Now I know this guy was just trying to save his own neck, but I had to explain the situation to him. "That's not how this works, man," I said. "To do crowd work, you need . . . a crowd."

"We aren't paying you if you don't do what you're contracted to do, which is perform between bands."

I proceeded to do ninety minutes of crowd work to an entirely empty field.

Those years were fun, frustrating, confusing, uncertain, humiliating, and everything I'd ever wanted my life to be. One of the adjectives that this stretch definitely wasn't was "easy." These money gigs I found were sometimes simple ("Come do improv at a restaurant on the Jersey Shore and we'll give you three hundred dollars and as much seafood as you can eat."), sometimes infuriating ("Hey, Animal Planet wants to expand into scripted comedy. I know, it's going to surprise *everyone*. Anyway, we're shooting a spec script. Will you do it for free? It shoots on Christmas Eve."), and sometimes just bizarre ("MTV is doing a show about trucks. Can you write jokes for it? You know, trucks. Garbage trucks, fire trucks, trucks. No, I don't know what that has to do with MTV.").

But they were jobs, small things that let me keep pursuing my dream. Little embers lit up, there for me to fan them. It was exciting to realize that all over this city were odd jobs that might allow me to cobble together an existence and a career in comedy. They weren't always aboveboard, many of them weren't great for the ego, and sometimes I'd get stiffed on the cash . . . but they were out there.

But they weren't enough.

Just under a year after my therapist told me to "give myself no other option," the money ran out. If the landlord had knocked on the door that minute, I'd have had to dip into my "break glass in case of emergency" two grand. I spent that night on a couch, shrugging off my girlfriend as she tried to console me, unable to even verbalize that I had broken my self-set boundaries. My dream was over. It was painful, but . . . I felt free. Now that my dreams had been ripped off like a Band-Aid, I could move on. I could try anything else.

That was a Tuesday night. On Friday, I booked my first role in a movie, which paid me enough to get through the end of the year and, eventually, led to my first big break—and first big failure—in Hollywood.

Am I a melodramatic person? Sometimes. Am I spiritual? Vaguely, and inconsistently. Do I think that life was handing me a lesson, saying *Hey kid, now that you showed us you were in fact ready to starve/be homeless for this we will allow it to actually happen*? One hundred percent abso-fucking-lutely.

The movie was *The Other Guys*. It starred Mark Wahlberg and Will Ferrell. You have maybe seen it on a plane at some point. Next time you're flying, you may notice toward the end of the movie a nerdy banker who has numerous guns pointed at his head. That's me.

Though I don't have many lines, shooting my scene was complicated. It took two days to film. It was an action scene, and filming action scenes is boring. There's a lot of resetting cameras to get a million different angles and it can get tedious. People tend to get bored in these situations, make jokes, whatever. This led to a lot of idiocy, but also a couple of cool stories.

Cool story number one: Before one take, Mark Wahlberg was holding a gun to my head and there was a delay before the director called action. The tedium of the day was setting in. People's energy was draining, and restlessness was setting in. As we sat waiting for the call, Wahlberg yelled, "TIC TAC."

I looked around at the other actors. Like me, they were confused, and the crew had raised eyebrows.

Wahlberg spoke again, even louder this time. "TIC TAC!"

"Umm . . . excuse me," I said. "Are you calling me Tic Tac?"

"No," Wahlberg replied. "Why would I call you Tic Tac?"

"I don't know, that's what I was wondering."

Now it was Wahlberg's turn to be confused. "Why would you even think I was calling you Tic Tac?"

"Um . . . I guess mostly because you were holding a fucking gun to my temple, looking me in the eye, and shouting the words 'Tic Tac'?"

I was tired, and this came off more disrespectful than I'd intended. The room went a bit still as everyone wondered to themselves, *Did that nerdy glorified extra just mouth off to Wahlberg?*

Wahlberg himself looked me up and down, then let out a breath and said, "I was asking my assistant to bring me a Tic Tac. But you know what, motherfucker? Now I *am* gonna call you Tic Tac."

And for the rest of the day, he did. Relentlessly. He let Will Ferrell know I was only to be referred to as Tic Tac. Everyone on set obeyed. PAs would approach—"Do you need a bottle of water or anything, Mr. Tic Tac?" The director, Adam McKay, was seated in what's called video village, a collection of monitors far from the set where the action can be viewed. Because of this distance he had to use a public address system to give us notes and call action.

"Will, this next take, maybe a little less aggressive and a little more puppy dog. And Mark, really go big with the anger, let's see if we can bounce those things off each other. And Tic Tac, you're doing a good job sitting there in silence. Keep doing that, Tic Tac. You're nailing it."

The day culminated when Michael Keaton arrived on set in advance of his night shoot. We were all sitting around as the cameras reset when he quietly walked in. Now, he seems to be a perfectly nice and unassuming man, but I was born in 1980 and there is no way around the fact that it's *Michael Keaton*. And I wasn't the only one—there was a reverence for the guy I could sense from all the way across the room, a respect everyone displayed.

Everyone except Mark Wahlberg.

"Yo, BATMAN!" he shouted from one end of the room up to the balcony where Michael Keaton was watching the action. It was a record-scratch moment. Everyone stopped. "BATMAN, this motherfucker—"

He pointed to me.

"—is named TIC TAC. He is only to be referred to as TIC TAC. By everybody. Even you, BATMAN."

Cool story number two: At the end of the shoot, Will Ferrell and Adam McKay were standing at video village watching back some footage, when I walked by.

"Hey, Tic Tac," Adam said. "Come here a minute."

Now, I didn't know Will or Adam before this shoot. I got the part because they needed a reader in the auditions. This is someone who isn't auditioning, but who sits next to the director and reads the lines so the actor who *is* auditioning has some-one to talk to. Adam wanted someone with improv chops. After my agent heard that, my agent got me the gig. I spent two days helping out other actors as they auditioned for parts in the film. That's all I expected it to be. But I guess I made McKay laugh a couple of times, because he tossed me this two-line nerdy banker role.

When they stopped me, I assumed I was getting fired. *Look, Michael Keaton's insecure about all the Batman stuff,* I figured they were about to say. *And we know it wasn't you, it was Wahlberg. But we can't fire fucking Wahlberg, he's fucking Wahlberg. So you're out, Tic Tac.*

Instead, Will said to me, "You're funny."

When Will Ferrell tells you you're funny, you have a few thoughts. *Wow* is the first one. And *He's just being nice* is the second.

Adam followed it up and said, "You're a good actor, too. Good stuff today."

Those kind words really fueled me and kept me going. On the practical side, it didn't hurt that the movie paid enough to get me through the next few months.

Early the next year, Ferrell and McKay were producing a show for Comedy Central. A few weeks before filming was set to begin, the lead, Jon Heder of *Napoleon Dynamite* fame, dropped out. To replace him, they auditioned ten actors. I was one of them.

I assume that conversation went as follows:

"Hey, Will Ferrell, we lost our lead actor, we're kinda fucked."

"I hear ya, Adam McKay, but I have an idea. We should get that kid . . . Candy Cane . . ."

"What are you talking about?"

"No . . . it was . . . shit. Life Saver? Was his name Life Saver?"

"Who in the fuck are you talking about?"

"That sad nerd with the giant forehead."

"OHHHHH, Tic Tac. Sure, let's give him a shot."

I auditioned. It came down to me and one other guy. I got the part.

An explosion of enthusiasm surrounded me. Blogs based in New York ran articles saying things like "In the local comedy underground this guy's been a hero forever; now the world's going to find out!" National publications sank their teeth into the idea that this unknown kid was replacing a bona fide movie star on just a few days' notice. The *New York Times* sent a reporter to the set and he wrote a profile on me titled "The Unlikely Pressures of Being a Sitcom Star." After a decade of toiling away in obscurity, my star didn't just rise, it exploded into the sky.

Landing the show also made me more money than I'd ever made in my life. Here's what I did with the biggest windfall of cash I'd ever seen by a factor of ten:

1. I bought two shirts and one pair of jeans from H&M.

2. For the first time in my life I bought prescription sunglasses.

3. I stuffed all the rest of it into a savings account and pretended it did not exist.

I changed nothing about my standard of living. All I did was make that "break glass in case of emergency" fund significantly larger. It went from two grand to a lot more than two grand. It meant that if things went bad I could last a year instead of a month this time.

And, oh, did things go bad. The show was a stinker from the start. It stumbled out of the gate and fell on its face. When I landed the part, I felt the love of the press and the public as their curiosity placed me on a pedestal. Just a few short months later, I learned what happens once you tumble from that pedestal.

A reporter writing about the show asked me the mortifying question "So many of your friends from the UCB Theatre have gone on to such great success—how does it feel to be the first one to drop the ball?" That wasn't easy. The reviews slamming the show almost always singled me out as the primary reason it did not work. Some of them were venomous. Those hurt. Some delighted in condescending pithiness that picked apart my performance. Those made me mad. But the worst were the ones that feigned sympathy with lines like "We have heard through the grapevine that Gethard is passably proficient at comedy. This vehicle makes that assertion seem false and for his sake we pray he gets another chance." Those *terrified* me.

The opinions of the lawless hordes of the faceless internet were just as brutal. I received random tweets from total strangers telling me I was talentless and ugly, and one even said that I deserved to die. Someone left a comment on the message board attached to my IMDb profile encouraging my agent to kill herself.

I understand that at this juncture you're probably thinking to yourself, *If this is a book where a dude who has met with some success encourages me, the reader, to find my own success, why the fuck is he bitching about a failure that's almost a decade old involving some show I've never even heard of? Stop whining about that and get to the good stuff.*

This is a reasonable reaction. I know that if you crave success, you want to read about the secrets to success, not some guy's biggest failure.

But if you ask me, failure *is* the secret to success. The road to your dreams is paved with asphalt that's composed of a combination of your fear, shame, desperation, and misery. This is not a book that will teach you how to hit a home run. It shows you instead how to become *world class* at striking out.

To my core, I identify as a proud loser. That being said, I'm aware that at this point in my life I've experienced a fair amount of success. Some of you picked up this book because you're fans of *The Chris Gethard Show* on truTV. Having a television show with your name in the title doesn't exactly scream "failure." Many of you purchased these writings because you enjoy my podcast, *Beautiful/Anonymous*. That show gets downloaded more than a hundred thousand times per episode, and when I tour it on the road, hundreds of people buy tickets. Maybe you're a fan of *Career Suicide*, a one-man show I performed on HBO that Judd Apatow produced. Sometimes people recognize me from acting roles I've landed. In middle America people very often approach me and say, "Didn't you play Dwight's assassin friend on *The Office*?" When I'm on college campuses or in "woke" coastal cities, they more often go with "Aren't you Ilana's boss on *Broad City*?"

I understand that this is hardly the résumé of a failure. It's the résumé of a hustler, someone who's had hard work meet with lucky breaks. So if I recognize the success in my professional life these days, why promote failure instead? I know that I have respect and options now, and I make a decent chunk of change each year that seemed impossible to earn even half a decade ago. So why would I tell you—as I'm about to for the next couple hundred pages—that your job isn't actually to learn how to win, but to lose well? Because I got to where I am today when I stopped chasing success and let the inner truth of my loser nature rise to the surface. I struggled for years, came close, struggled some more, finally had some things happen, and still lost. Even today, I still feel like I'm failing on a near daily basis. My success was not handed to me, nor was it built in a traditional way. It was born in a dusty, strange public access studio. My success only happened when I ignored advice I knew was good and made choices I was certain were ill-advised.

Some people are born with movie-star good looks and endless charisma and charm. I assume any of those people who picked up this book have already tossed it aside. The rest of us are journeymen. You and me, our lives have problems. Our confidence will never be much to write home about. Our doubts define us. But we're willing to get our fucking hands dirty as long as someone can give us a reason we shouldn't quit. These are my people, and I want this book to be that reason.

The art of success isn't the art of succeeding; it's the art of survival. And survival isn't something you get great at by winning. It's perfected only through bitter, brutal, and beautiful defeat.

Put another way: success isn't always successful, and failure can sometimes secretly be success.

I once did a press junket to promote the aforementioned sitcom. A press junket means you wear fancy clothes and go to a room where reporters are shuffled in one after the other to ask you questions. You're supposed to give answers that promote the company line and get people to buy what you're selling, or in my case, watch the television show I'm appearing in. The reporters come in, mumble which publication they're from, and then you get into it. They ask questions they've asked a hundred times before. You give answers you've given a hundred times before. We all move on with our lives.

For this particular press junket, a fancy car was sent to my house in Queens to bring me into Manhattan. My car was fancy, my clothes were fancy. I was feeling like a pretty fancy boy that day. I tried to leave my house and the doorknob fell off in my hand. I still don't know how. It's not like I was more forceful than usual or anything, and even if I was, I am not superhuman. I'm not even average strong. I don't have the ability to rip a doorknob off a door. But sure enough, there it was, in my palm.

I couldn't leave my house.

I tried to reattach the doorknob. No dice. I'm good with jokes, but screwdrivers have always eluded me. Panic set in. They sent a car for one express reason—it was not okay to be late to a day like this. People had poured millions of dollars into this show. The least I could do was be on time.

I sprinted to my bedroom, opened my window, and crawled onto the fire escape. I got to the bottom only to find that the mechanism that released the ladder to the ground didn't work. So I jumped.

I landed in a giant pile of garbage bags.

A sitcom gig. A fancy car. Press interviews, ego stroking.

That's not how I remember that day at all. In my mind, that will always be the day I jumped into a pile of garbage.

On the other side of the coin, I once drove cross-country with some of my comedian friends in an RV. We were making videos from the road every day. We thought these videos were going to set the world on fire. We saw real viral potential. Instead, no one particularly cared about them. It was dismal, being out there on the road in the middle of nowhere knowing we were falling on our faces one video at a time.

We rolled into Taos, New Mexico, feeling pretty demoralized. I knew nothing of Taos when we entered. Turns out it's a strange place, made up of rich people who like skiing and live in multi-million-dollar homes and surreal hippie artists who like living off the grid.

We wound up eating in a tiny restaurant on top of a mountain. No one else was there so we got talking with the cook and waiter, who were the only employees there that night. These guys were spaced out in a major way. They seemed like they had molly for breakfast and mushrooms for lunch. They told us about Taos, about how it was visited by aliens, about how the hot springs in town had mystical healing powers.

Then they asked what we did. We told them we were comedians and they invited us to put on a show in their house that night. They said they'd invite all their friends.

We had nothing to lose.

Turns out their house wasn't a house at all, it was a yurt. A yurt is a Mongolian-style tent, and that's where these guys lived. We wandered into the yurt. They were there with a girl we hadn't met before. They'd invited everyone in town, but she was the only friend who took them up on their offer for a free comedy show. She brought a dog.

That night I did a show in a yurt for three humans and a dog, and it is one of the best shows I've ever done. I don't know how to explain it. I've certainly done better-attended shows (the most people I've performed live for at once is twelve thousand). I've done shows in legendary venues, in cities filled with industry professionals.

But that night, those three hippies and that dog laughed harder than they'd ever laughed before and I felt every drop of dopamine in my brain come to life.

I wouldn't trade that show for anything.

Sometimes success means sitting in a pile of garbage, and sometimes failure means you get to put on the best show of your life.

I can tell you with great honesty—my life doesn't look anything like the life I envisioned for myself. It's taken multiple twists and turns, and it wasn't always easy. Don't get me wrong. Before you roll your eyes too hard and think to yourself, *Okay, suburban white television man*, I'm very much aware that things worked out pretty well for me. But in the beginning of my journey I saw a much more traditional career in my future. Ask anyone who's at all aware of my work and they will tell you, "He is many things, but traditional isn't one of them." I wanted ego-soothing fame. I craved validation. Now I make a significant chunk of my income via an often-sad podcast and a television show so weird that I regularly read internet comments along the lines of "Why does this nerd with the big head claim that shirtless dude is a fish creature from the sea?" It's some version of success but not the one I craved—not by a long shot. I can remember what I wanted at the starting line, and I can see where I'm at now, and I can say that I have landed somewhere that me in 2007 would have called "reasonably okay." And that's fine. It's where I'm supposed to be—and I want to help you get to where you're supposed to be by showing you how I, a self-identifying loser, learned to master my own bitter, brutal, and beautiful defeats while pursuing my dreams.

I want you to know that I believe in you.

Some caveats:

First: I don't really know you. You are at this point an abstract thought to me, a theoretical reader who has purchased, borrowed, or stolen this book at some point far in the future. That being said—I believe in you. Because you are a human being and you have some latent ambition inside you that remains unacted upon. I think that ambition can come out and should come out. In fact, not only do I think you have a right to put it into action, I think you have a responsibility to do so.

A second caveat: While I believe in you, I absolutely do not believe in your ability to succeed. Far from it. You are going to fail. Of this, I am certain. You're going to unlock your ambition and it's going to betray you; you're going to fall right on your face. You're going to put a plan into action and it will end in humiliation, or even worse, be met with nothing but ice-cold apathy. You're going to waste your savings chasing a dream. You're going to strike out. Lose. Come up short. That's the statistical likelihood, and only a scant few of you are going to defy those numbers, break out, and make something happen. Prove me wrong. I want you to. But my guess is, most of you are going to lose. To the extent that I believe in you, I only believe in your right and responsibility to fail.

But here's a secret—once you do, you'll be fine.

Though I don't believe in your ability to succeed, I do believe in your right to try. I do believe in your ability to land where you're supposed to be, whether it's a garbage pile or a Mongolian tent. I think if you fall into either of those, you'll take some unexpected bumps and bruises. But I also think you'll wind up okay.

I don't think you can change the world. But I do think you can change *your* world, in subtle ways, small ways, ways that remain internal and known only to you.

You'll feel good about it. Trust me. You'll be a happy failure shaking off the shame of public embarrassment and you will feel so much better about that than you do right now, harboring secret desires and hopes that you refuse to act upon because you're scared.

I'm never going to tell you to make a vision board. I can't give you "seven simple steps" to anything. What I can say is that if you're feeling frustrated with how things are, the best way to change them might just be to crash and burn, to flame out in disastrous fashion. If you can stop fearing failure and learn to treat failure as a trusted friend, you might just wind up feeling a little more okay than you used to. I don't think you'll achieve your goals, but you'll at least disrupt the status quo. And that's something.

We fear failure. Our instinct is to avoid it. We have this faint feeling that failure is like a fire that will burn everything down.

It is. That's why you need to go for it. When you're standing in the ashes, terrified and overwhelmed—that's when your life may actually begin. Forest fires promote positive regrowth. Sometimes, failure does too.

Some people might call that self-defeatism, but I like to call it productive realism. A lot of people sell you a false bill of goods where the world winds up smelling like roses. I'm selling you the idea of a world that often smells firmly of shit, but where that shit becomes fertilizer that makes good things grow.

Set the bar a little lower. Get the phrase "aim high" out of your head. Aim realistic and don't beat yourself up if you can't even get there. And be humble if you somehow wind up being one of the lucky few who somehow manage to exceed it.

For example, this book:

As I'm writing this, I have a pretty clear idea of some broad potential outcomes. I can see the dream, I can see the nightmare, and I can see the outcome I'd be reasonably okay with.

Let's start with the nightmare: This book comes out, gets brutally slammed in the press, and even the existing fans of my work don't buy it. The publisher gives me panicked phone calls where we all stress and wonder at the level of disaster we're experiencing. It is so bad that people who have been fans of my other work for years flee even from that because the stink of this book now pervades everything about me. I feel bad that trees were killed to make this. I have to give my advance back, an unprecedented move that I don't argue with due to my vast sea of Irish-Catholic guilt. I can't pay my mortgage. My car gets repossessed. My wife and I have a frank conversation where she tells me she still loves me but that we can't survive unless we split up and fend for ourselves. She moves on and settles down with another guy. They have a kid. I drink in gutters. I sell myself for drugs. Every Christmas I sneak onto a train and make my way to the suburbs. I creep up to my ex-wife's house and watch her kid open presents on Christmas morning. They look so happy. They look so warm. She hears a noise and looks up. By the time she gets to the door, I am gone. Was she imagining it? No. There are tracks in the snow.

The dream: This book is an immediate sensation. Six weeks after it's published it is assigned by mandatory federal decree to every high school curriculum in the nation. It is the new *To Kill a Mockingbird*, but focusing on life advice delivered by an unqualified man instead of rich character development and a stark look at the racial divide of American society. I am a literary celebrity on a level unseen since Truman Capote. Like him, I start throwing parties for New York society and bring together the old-money Fifth Avenue crowd and the new school artists who will redefine our future. At one of these parties I pay to have a docile tiger sit purring atop a white grand piano. At the peak of the party I stand on a lectern and announce that my time in this world is over. Like the elves at the end of the Lord of the Rings trilogy, I put on a robe and walk through the woods and hum and chant and head to a mystical land where I and people who look like Liv Tyler live forever.

I'm pretty certain neither of those is going to happen. So here's where I'm setting the bar. Here's what *losing well* looks like: You buy this book and leave it next to your toilet. You read it when you can, but it's kind of come and go because you've got a lot going on. Sometimes at night you get gassy and things take a little while, so you're able to really sink your teeth into it. On those nights you're like, *That's a pretty good read.*

Anything that exceeds that, woo hoo. If it comes in below that, at least I know I went for something. I won't feel bad for myself; I will only weep for the trees.

Most of all—if you're reading this on a toilet right now, at two a.m. because you ate too much too close to bedtime, I'm happy I just blew your mind.

LOSE WELL

The most underestimated source of power is losing.

This seems counterintuitive, I know. When it comes to winning or losing, winning is always the goal, while losing is to be avoided—at all costs. This stigmatizes losing and robs it of its power as a learning tool.

We live in a culture where there appear to be two options: win or lose. Because of this, we often fall into the trap of pursuing a hidden, insidious third option. We don't chase the glory of the win. Instead, we set out to *not lose*. This is one of the most detrimental behaviors to achieving a desired goal. Not losing is not the same as winning.

The goal isn't to avoid losing. The goal is learning how to lose well.

So get good at losing.

Losing thickens your skin. Losing exposes the dead ends. Losing teaches resilience. Losing the first time highlights a more viable path for your second pass. You have to learn to lose. You have to embrace the bomb. You have to follow the fear.

The key to getting ahead is losing, painfully, over and over again. Success requires hard work. But it also needs luck. The most successful people I know are incredibly talented and relentlessly hard workers. They also got incredibly lucky. Never mistake luck for success, though they often go hand in hand. Luck is a random win. To handle unexpected luck, you need to first experience a proud legacy of losses that prepare you for newfound success. When you finally do win, an outside observer will never be able to understand that this out-of-the-blue success is, at heart, just an unexpected and pleasant positive outcome in the middle of a long pattern of failure you've been practicing for years.

Think of a train rumbling past you at full speed. Success is climbing onto it. To board the train, your muscles need to be strong, your senses need to be sharp, and your timing needs to be perfect. It is not realistic to think that the first time the train rolls by you'll be able to do this. Hobos do it all the time. These people literally eat beans out of cans. If they can make it happen, you should be able to do it too. Eventually. The only way to learn how is to willingly fall down many times in the effort. This will bring you perilously close to getting ground up on the tracks. The more you fall, though, the less terrifying that idea becomes. When the fear of falling goes away and you begin to understand just what kind of bruises falling incurs, you will find that one day, seemingly out of nowhere, you wind up jumping on the train. Winning out of the gate isn't realistic; in fact, it's arrogant. Losing is the only thing you can do right now, the present practice that lets you achieve future success when the opportunity arises.

Every loss is a lesson. If you can adjust your mentality, where you no longer fear losing but start to embrace it, you will be a battle-scarred, weathered, ironclad machine ready to handle success once it arrives.

Losing makes our muscles strong.

As an exercise, I want you to think of three times when you've felt like an absolute loser. These can be from any area of your life. Personal. Professional. Public or private. Remember three times where at your core, you felt like you'd struck out. Times where you felt exposed, where you felt like the world beat you down.

Lucky for me, I have a lot of options to choose from. I have always been a loser. I will always be a loser. I'm good at being a loser, because I've had a lot of practice.

It's 1992, and I just asked a girl to dance. *This is a big deal.* I'm in sixth grade. Her name is Tatiana. She's tall and pretty, a blonde with a great smile. Her older brother is named Fabio. She's cool. I'm about nine inches shorter than her. My sweater is too tight. My glasses are too big. My last name spells out the words *Get Hard*. I should not be dating anyone who comes from a family that names their children "Tatiana" and "Fabio." But I still went for it.

It wasn't an easy decision. Word had gotten out weeks earlier that I liked Tatiana. Guys in my class egged me on: *There's a dance coming up. Ask her!* I did. She said she'd think about it. Before Tatiana got back to me with an answer, my mom found out and said I wasn't old enough to ask a girl out. I had to rescind my generous offer, which saved me a surefire rejection.

Back at the dance, like all sixth-grade boys, I hug the wall. The hours tick by. We joke among ourselves. We dedicate Ugly Kid Joe's "I Hate Everything About You" to the people in our class we don't like. It is everything a sixth-grade dance should be.

"Unchained Melody" plays. Standard "end of the dance" fare for a middle-school setting.

David Peter approaches me. "Go ask Tatiana to dance," he says.

This makes no sense. I am not friends with David Peter. There's no reason he should be doing anything for me. All I know about David Peter is that when I was in fourth grade, our town held a mile run. He got first place and I got second—easily, to this day, the greatest athletic achievement of my life. This conversation is the longest he and I have ever had and would ever have.

"I don't want to," I tell him. "Also, you and I aren't friends, so I'm not sure why you—"

"Dude, I requested this song so you could ask her to dance," he says. He places his hand on my shoulder and looks deep into my eyes. "Go get it done."

I now feel like if I don't ask Tatiana to dance I will let down this kid David whose opinion means nothing to me. To someone raised Irish-Catholic, that kind of guilt is unbearable.

The sea parts, and I approach Tatiana.

"Will you, uh . . ."

She stares at me.

"Dance . . . with me?"

"Sure," she says, completely devoid of any emotion. She's getting it over with.

I don't know where to place my hands. She holds my shoulders. I hold her waist. My sweater meets her tiger print dress. I feel my khakis tighten. I have a sixth-grade boner.

There's a tap on my shoulder. I am not expecting this. It's Mikey O'Connell, an eighth grader with a mullet and a pierced ear. Mikey is cool and dangerous. I once saw him drive a car through my neighborhood, without an adult present, even though he is a child.

"Let me cut in," he says. He does not ask. It's a statement. I'm stunned. I step back. Mikey slides in. Tatiana smiles. She's way more into him than me. I turn, shock in my face. The boys from my class, who continue to hug the wall, point and laugh at me. I look down. My boner is visible.

I sprint from the gym to the bathroom. I lock myself in a stall and I cry. Tears fall. I try to keep it inaudible even though I'm heaving with emotion. The door opens. I hold my breath.

"Chris?"

I stay quiet.

"Chris, I know you're in here," the voice continues. "It's Danny."

Danny Tobia is the coolest kid in my class, possibly the coolest kid in school.

"I saw what happened out there," he tells me through the stall door. "Unacceptable. I let Mikey O know that it wasn't cool. He's out of the picture. The song's still playing. Tatiana wants to dance with you."

I don't come out. I hear him leave. I take a few deep breaths, kick open the stall door, and wash my face in the sink. My eyes are pink. My face is red. But I know what I have to do.

As I reenter the gym, I see Tatiana standing at center court. Everyone's watching. This is a middle-school dance, so there are laser lights and disco balls. It is bright. Everyone can tell that I've been crying. I walk up to her.

"Hi," I say.

"Hey," she answers. She's still emotionless.

We resume dancing. Eleven seconds later the song ends.

"Bye," she says. She turns and walks away.

I walk home by myself.

On Monday, Jeff Chang tells me that on the bus to school that morning, Tatiana said she felt my boner through my pants. She called me a pig. We never spoke again.

It is now 2001. I'm freezing behind the glass deli counter at an A&P supermarket, which has only been open for less than a month. I'm twenty-one years old and I only got this job because the store management was willing to hire anyone for their initial launch. Convicts, people whose names are almost definitely aliases, and other alcoholic college kids like me, my brother, and a handful of our goony friends. We are spending the summer in our depressing college town of New Brunswick, New Jersey. I have no money, no fake ID, and not much going for me. My girlfriend is in Italy. Before she left, we decided that because we've been dating since we were seventeen we should probably have an open summer and make out with other people. In the months since, I have managed to make out with zero people. She emailed me that she'd made out with more than one smooth Italian guy. It is not a fun summer.

An elderly lady approaches the counter. I have nothing but respect and love for my elders, but as people get older, they start to view deli employees as their natural enemies. The older a person gets, the thinner they want their meat sliced. This is a fact. I was warned about this very thing during my training. "If you see a walker," my manager told me, "cut that meat thin. Those old fuckers never stop." This was the most useful piece of my training, even more important than the actual instructions about how to operate the slicing machines.

The woman is shorter than the counter. She blinks at me from behind huge, thick lenses. Her oversize purse hangs over her shoulder, and she clutches her walker as she peers into our case. She's adorable. But I am still leery.

"I want a half a pound of the Genoa hard salami," she tells me. She pauses and looks me right in the eye. *"And slice it thin."*

Curveball: we do not carry a product called Genoa hard salami.

"Ma'am, I'm a little confused," I say. "We have Genoa salami. And we have hard salami. But we do not have Genoa hard salami."

"Of course you do," she says matter-of-factly.

"Uhh . . . there's nothing called that. I'm looking at our two types of salami here, okay? You can read the labels. This one says Genoa. This one says hard."

"Don't tell me about salami," she says. "I've been eating salami for seven decades."

She trembles a little. I realize she is tensing up for a fight.

"Ma'am, I'm sure you're right. I'm positive that the one marked Genoa salami must be the one you want. Should we go with that?"

"Well, is it Genoa *hard*?" she asks.

"Honestly? I have no idea. I've only worked here for three weeks."

She stands on her tiptoes and leans over the counter and summons me toward her. To make eye contact, I have to lean on the counter. Then this teeny tiny woman—somebody's grandma—looks me right in the eye and says, "I see the game you're playing. *You don't want to fuck with me.*"

I am flummoxed.

"I don't know what you want me to tell you," I say. "We only have the salamis we have. I can't summon a new kind of salami out of thin air."

"Give me the fucking Genoa," she snarls.

I reach for the salami. I pick it up. It has been shaved down. We're down to its final twenty percent. Nobody likes that final chunk of salami. Nobody. This is not good. We're already at Defcon One, and she is going to view the tail end of a salami as an act of war. I try to get out ahead of this.

With the care of a lion tamer in the middle of his act, I gently say, "Ma'am, we're down to the nub on this one. I'm going to head to the freezer and grab a fresh salami. You'll get the first crack at a new one that I'll open right now."

She does not hear me. I do not blame her. She is very old. Hearing is one of the first things to go. All she sees is the nub as I hold it up. She's done. Her face turns red. This is rage.

"YOU," she shouts, "CAN GO FUCK YOURSELF."

"Hey!" I shout. "You need to calm down!"

She grabs her walker and stomps away, as much as one can stomp away behind a walker.

Half an hour later, the general manager of the store approaches me.

"Chris," he says, "is it true you yelled at a customer today?"

"Yeah," I say. "It was nuts. She told me to go fuck myself. I told her to calm down."

"Don't ever do that again," he tells me. "You don't ever yell at a customer again."

"She told me to go fuck myself!" I say. "I was just trying to stand up for myself."

"We don't do that at A&P!" he tells me. "We do *not* stand up for ourselves here!"

He leaves. I grab the nub of Genoa salami. I enter the freezer and sit on a wooden crate filled with endless amounts of disgusting head cheese. I have no money and can't stomach the thought of eating a cheap packet of Ramen another night this week. Shivering in the cold, I bite into the sad little salami nub. It is not the first or last time I ate questionable meat while hiding in an A&P freezer.

It's 2014. I'm on my honeymoon. Hawaii. The Big Island. It's amazing. And so is my wife, Hallie. She's talented and smart and funny and kind and gorgeous and I can't believe she shacked up with a goon like me.

Our honeymoon is beautiful. It's incredible. But it also involves "me doing a series of things that I am terrified to do." My wife loves activities. Anything that one can do, she wants to do. Put it in a brochure and leave it in a rack in a hotel lobby and she wants to sign up pronto.

My wife is fearless. I am not. But I am in love, and I do not want to spoil anything about this once-in-a-lifetime vacation, this inaugural celebration of our love.

We zip-line through a jungle canopy. It's breathtaking, but I'm convinced the whole time that my harness is going to break and I am going to die.

We ride horses through a valley. It's indescribably pretty, but

I'm convinced my horse will sense my fear, buck me off, and before I hit the ground kick me in the head, killing me on the spot.

We find out that due to some strange interaction between volcanic ash and ocean water, there's a beach with green sand. My wife *has* to see the green sand. To get to this beach, however, one must hike through sand dunes. We hike in the wrong direction and are lost for less than fifteen minutes. During those fifteen minutes, I am convinced that I'm going to dehydrate and die. Luckily, two spoiled Russian lovers in their early twenties wearing designer track pants come to our rescue. (They tell us that Hawaii has not lived up to the hype. Paris did not live up to the hype. Tokyo did not live up to the hype. The only city they've ever visited that met their expectations? "Washington, DC," the Russian dude tells us. "Greatest fucking city in the fucking world.")

Each activity pushes my anxiety to the brink. But because love trumps everything, even fear, I do all of it.

So when Hallie tells me we should go on a "late-night manta ray swim," I tell her I'm all for it. We get on a boat after dark. This already freaks me out. I wear a wet suit. We make our way out into the ocean, where she and I and about a dozen other dummy tourists dive into the sea and hold on to an oversize surfboard with handles. The leaders of this tour shine spotlights into the depths. The light attracts massive manta rays, which are a dozen feet wide. They swim inches from our faces. They dive down deep, then swim upward toward us, their mouths open so wide that we can see into their insides. They're old and special and both Hallie and I are on the verge of tears seeing them, though I also scream in fear every time one enters my peripheral vision.

It also involves a lot of bobbing. We are in the water for over an hour, clutching those handles and just bobbing, bobbing, bobbing with the sea. We get back on the boat and I know right away that something is wrong. Dizziness sets in. I feel a churn overtake my stomach. I say nothing. I've been married for three days. I can't have my wife knowing how weak I am. (She definitely already knows.)

Back onshore, I peel off my wet suit in record time and bolt for the car. Hallie follows at a normal human pace.

"Let'sgetbacktoourairbandbasquickaswecanitwasromantic," I blurt out in a panic.

As soon as her door shuts I throw our rented SUV into gear and skid out of there. The place we are staying is at the bottom of a steep hill and, to get there, we have to take curving, narrow, poorly lit roads. Hawaii isn't huge on safety. They don't have guardrails (or lifeguards). I don't hit the brakes once going around those curves. I'm racing my own weak stomach. Hallie has no idea.

"Baby," she finally says, "you should probably slow down a little bit."

"Yeahofcoursenoproblemmmmm," I mumble. Then I skid to the side of the road, throw the car in park, and tumble out of the driver's-side door.

I know vomit is coming. Hard and fast. I go into panic mode and look for the right spot to puke. I run about fifteen feet and start vomiting directly in front of our parked SUV. That's when I realize that in my rush to get out of the car I forgot to turn off the engine. The SUV's headlights are shining right on me, and my beautiful new bride is watching me as I puke, hard, five times, like some kind of dying animal.

And then I remember I'm wearing a fancy pair of sneakers that I usually only wear while performing special shows in order to give myself a kick of confidence. I take a deep breath and throw up directly on them. I turn my head, squint into the headlights, and wonder if my new wife is still watching.

Those are just three examples of times I felt like a total hard-core loser. There are many more. You have yours.

Some loser moments will always sting. When I think about Mikey O'Connell cutting in, it still burns in my core even though that took place years before Green Day formed. I remember the sadness of sitting in a freezer eating garbage meat, of puking on my own shoes. The feelings those memories bring up are still visceral and raw to me. The emotional gut punch will never totally leave my system.

But I can also laugh at those experiences. With the benefit of time, they become funny, entertaining stories to share. By remembering them, I can let the pain coexist with humor and joy. And for the life of me, I can't think of any time I've ever been a loser that hasn't sharpened a weapon in my arsenal in some meaningful, lasting way.

My first dance saw an older kid cut in. That taught me a little bit about standing up for myself. I got embarrassed, removed from a dance in front of all my middle-school peers. I'd go on to strike out with women many more times, but I learned to show a little backbone, be direct, and not run at the first sign of insecurity. That incident became a little blip woven into the DNA of how I viewed myself and how I wanted to move forward. Its effects weren't evident in the moment, but over time even that disaster helped me.

I spent about a week feeling guilty about yelling at somebody's grandma. I ran back our encounter frequently in my mind. Even though she'd been pretty unreasonable from the start, nobody wants to send a cute old lady into a blind rage. Could I have done anything differently? Yes. I could have communicated more clearly. I could have spoken more loudly, been more direct, I could have let my guard down and shared my confusion with her. I could have tried to charm her. I could have asked a supervisor to rescue me. There were half a dozen paths out of that situation that I failed to see in that moment. But through trial and error, I learned to recognize that such paths always exist and later would be smart enough to take one of those paths in the moment. Learning how to be versatile, how to find the options different conversations presented me with, how to sense the emotional tenor of people I was engaged with and the directions our conversations were taking—all this would serve me well over time, in environments that were a lot more treacherous than a supermarket deli counter. That little fight, coupled with my ability to analyze it, didn't teach me all that at once, but it certainly served as one of many building blocks that taught me how to interact with different types of people.

As for throwing up on my honeymoon, that was only a few years back and to be honest I'm still processing it. At the very least, I've learned one practical lesson—*Next time you gotta vomit your guts out in front of your wife, don't stand directly in a spotlight in her line of vision. And maybe aim like six inches to the left so you don't fuck up your cool-guy sneakers.* In all seriousness, I was reminded that my wife will love me through anything, that I should speak up when I'm under duress, and that I should more freely admit my own limitations.

Without these lessons, and thousands more I've learned over the years living and operating in the L column, I wouldn't have known how to handle the success my midthirties brought. When I was twenty years old, I chose to go after my dream of being a comedian. I'd wager that ninety-nine percent of the people holding this book never heard of me until I was about thirty-four—fourteen years after I started. To this day, some of you may only have a vague awareness of me. Some people only know one of my projects and are shocked to find others even exist. Fans of my podcast have been baffled to find out I have a television show. People who know me as a character actor are confused when they learn that I also have an HBO special. My career remains scattered and largely underground, but it now also has more momentum and tangible markers of success than ever before.

It's fair to say that things only got to this point—a shaky, disjointed, fun but tenuous career that feels sort of like a victory—after a decade and a half of trying and failing. I look back over that time and spot some fleeting stabs at success that came and went. But I see thousands of failures, and I can't think of one of them that didn't teach me something. After years of trying to jump on the train, I finally held on to the handle, but only because I kept failing until my losing attempts resulted in a win.

You want to get out there and go for it. That's great. Failure is your friend. Winning is your goal, or losing is your goal. You never want to land in that sad middle ground where you *haven't failed*. Where you did nothing to embarrass yourself, but didn't do anything to distinguish yourself either. That's the difference between winning and playing not to lose.

You want success. You want glory. You want to get over the hump and achieve what you've set out to do. Knowing failure is the only true way to understand success.

Lose. Lose proudly. Lose often. Lose well.

YOU ARE THE CHAOS

The only way to break a habit is to pick up a new one.

There are habits in your life holding you back. Maybe you're unable to find enough time to focus on your projects. Maybe you defer to the needs of someone else before thinking about your own needs. Maybe you wake up too late and it eats away hours in your day that could otherwise have been more productive. Maybe, like me, you waste too many hours a day farting around on social media. (Because the only thing more important than being productive is reading what your middle-aged former college roommates think about a *Star Wars* movie meant for children.)

As you embark upon the effort to make or do something that reflects your unfulfilled desires, those are things you'll want to change.

Easier said than done.

You have other habits, too, things that don't have a negative impact on your life. Maybe you eat the same thing for breakfast every morning. Maybe you always watch Netflix on your iPad in bed as you fall asleep. Maybe you call your mom to see how she's doing every Wednesday at noon. Things like this provide structure in your life and don't create roadblocks in any way.

Life functions best with order. I've seen too much footage of riots on television to feel like I can give total anarchy a thumbs-up. (A big part of this is that I am almost certain I wouldn't survive an apocalypse scenario. As soon as my glasses break—*dead*.)

Order is good. It's why the grocery store at the end of my block always has fresh produce. It's why I can click a few buttons on my computer and the next day some dude brings me an iPad stand, or whatever my ill-advised late-night panic purchase was in that particular instance. And on top of that, it's why we aren't spending all day every day fending off murderers and bandits in the streets.

That being said, order can also be a real drag. It's stifling. It's boring. And worst of all it sets us into routines. At first, these routines are a welcome part of life. Wake up at the same time. Drive the same route to work. Rotate the same four or five places for lunch because they serve what you like to eat.

Then the next thing you know, you hear yourself saying it out loud again. "Can I please have a six-inch turkey and ham on Italian herb and cheese bread?" And you have this moment where way deep in your brain you hear yourself scream, *If I ever order this shitty sandwich one more time, I'm going to kill myself.*

That voice comes and goes in an instant. We ignore it or stuff it down or laugh at it.

I encourage you to listen to it.

Right out of the gate, I AM NOT ENCOURAGING YOU TO KILL YOURSELF.

Now that that's out of the way, let's recognize that the voice exists. It screamed that dissatisfaction (or more likely your own version of it, as I assume not everyone's existential crisis unfolds in America's most tolerated fast-food sandwich shop). From time to time, it comes up, and I want you to act on it. I want you to let it stop you in your tracks. Every time you hear it rattle in the back of your brain, it's a chance to recognize that the routines, the regularity, the order have become a drag and some small piece of you wants to break your existing habits over your knee to see what's on the other side.

Life is order. You are the chaos.

This is your chance. Be the chaos. Breathe in deep and be the disruption to the routine.

Chaos is the feeling you have when you don't know how something's going to end. It's the feeling you have between placing the bet and seeing the finish line. It's unsafe. It triggers every self-defense instinct we have. Rules don't matter. Plans don't matter. You can only react to what's happening right now. You spend your whole life building routines and structures to hold them together. Chaos means kicking those things over, cutting the strings to the safety nets. Chaos is terrifying. It's also occasionally necessary.

Believe me, my day-to-day existence is quite boring. I've got a ton of routines. There's one restaurant in my neighborhood that lets me sit and write. Any time I go, I order a tuna melt and breakfast tea. It's boring. I wear striped shirts almost every day. I click refresh on the same eleven websites. My life is stable. I like it that way.

But I've felt a lot of frustration, too. There have been many moments of feeling shackled to the way things are when that doesn't seem to feel like how it's supposed to be. I've had long stretches where I've felt "meh" about my life because I was doing what I thought "people like me are supposed to do." I look back at these stretches and see weeks, months, sometimes years that weren't as happy as they could have been. During these stretches my decisions were guided by instincts I do not respect: fear, complacency, and insecurity. My routines felt safe. Because I was unwilling to disrupt them, I lived with my frustration and discontent. I was too scared to see what was on the other side.

These days, I'm happy. I do things I love, and I have breathing room in the ways that I need to keep my head on straight.

It wasn't always like this. The only reason I have these things is because I listened to the voice. That dim scream in the back of my head that said, *You hate this. You can change it.* When things were at their most grim, I heard it most often, and on a handful of occasions I chose to listen.

The voice said, "Go!"

I said, "Where?"

The voice said, "I haven't thought it out that far. Anywhere. Right now. If you don't do it now, you'll never do it."

I said, "This is terrifying, but . . . okay."

After years of sitting around hoping things would change, I stopped worrying about the consequences and made change happen.

Make a habit of destroying your bad habits. Sometimes it's easier to shake things up by breaking the harmless habits first. There is comfort in those habits, but that comfort is sometimes the biggest roadblock of all. And by breaking the habits that *don't* matter, you get yourself prepared to break the habits that do.

Instead of a smoothie every morning, maybe you go *fucking apeshit* one day and have a bagel with cream cheese. Maybe instead of Netflix, you fall asleep to a podcast for a few nights in a row. Maybe you call your mom at three this week as opposed to noon. She'll be fine waiting a few hours. Maybe email her first so she doesn't worry about whether something's wrong and overreact and call your sister in a panic wondering if you're dead in a ditch somewhere. Simple adjustments that bend your own rules teach you how to circumvent the things that seem insurmountable.

Once you've made a habit of breaking harmless habits, it will seem less daunting to break the harmful ones. They won't seem like great white whales that you have to spear and more like experiments that you get to participate in. Because they're the impediments to your success, you give them great weight. They become almost mythic in their power over you. Break that power by exposing them first. These are like mini Wizard of Oz moments you get to have in your own life; maybe that thing that seems superpowerful is just a meek little weirdo behind a curtain who at first glance sort of resembles Mel Brooks.

Once you're eating something different for breakfast every day, I bet you won't be so resistant to the idea of setting the alarm a bit earlier. The Netflix to podcast switch might have no effect, or the minor change in your routine might give you the confidence to start saying no to the people who eat up all your energy and time. Maybe calling your mom at random times instead of on a schedule will make you think differently about the idea of a schedule and will give you the breathing room to turn off your phone for a few hours, be a little more selfish, and carve out the time for yourself that you need.

My shrink has given me so much good advice over the years, which I will reiterate is awesome because I have given her a considerable chunk of change. One of the best pieces was simple—"Never walk home the same way twice." This sounds like the simplest thing in the world, but it had a profound effect on me.

At the time I lived on Sixty-Seventh Street in Woodside, Queens, which is conveniently located near a subway stop at Sixty-Ninth Street. There was no reason for me to ever go to a different train station. Except, of course, if I wanted to break my routine.

Every once in a while, I'd get off the train one stop earlier. I'd walk down different streets on my way home. I started waking up early some days just so I could walk farther to other subway stations. If I did go to Sixty-Ninth Street, I'd walk the long way around the block. In doing so, I found and stopped in restaurants I'd never eaten in before. One was this Chilean place with a sick-ass peach drink. I'd go to the dollar store on my way home, with no intention of buying anything. It was just to walk the aisles, to see things I wasn't planning on seeing that day. I never knew that dollar stores in Queens were like the World's Fuckin' Fair. There's a dollar store on the corner of Seventy-Eighth and Roosevelt that contains everything. I've never once gone in there and not gotten what I needed. *They even sell four-foot-wide dream catchers.*

By bending my life in the direction of directionlessness, I noticed two strong effects. First, I found that in general my eyes and ears were more open. While remembering that there are things all over this world that I don't know about, all the time, I committed to breaking out of the tunnel vision I had developed over the years. Why take the shortest route if you have extra time? Use those extra five minutes to experience something, anything.

This attitude soon extended to people as well. I saw others on the street and considered them in a different light. People were no longer just obstacles between me and my front door. They were my neighbors, members of my community. Though I would never unearth their stories, I reminded myself that every single person I passed had one. Everyone struggles. Everyone fights through something. That basic reminder of humanity, of being part of a larger world, had an effect not just on the quality of my work, but my desire to produce it.

At the same time, I soon found that I'd developed a new internal mantra: *This ten minutes is just for me.* I found that it was easy to find ten minutes each day where I could set my phone to airplane mode, where I could take some time for myself, where there was a stretch that wasn't for the benefit of my roommate, my wife, my boss, or anyone else. Those ten minutes were mine. And things happened during that ten minutes. Not game changers. Beautiful, inconsequential moments that no one else needs to know about. They were my secrets. Small secrets, sure, but in my sole possession more sacred than I ever expected.

Bad habits seem daunting and impossible to overcome. Good habits should be treasured. But we have dozens if not hundreds of hollow inconsequential habits in our lives. Those are simple to readjust, to lose, to move on from. By being the chaos, we create the most empowering habit of all—the habit of destroying our routines. Once this is committed to, those bad habits are exposed as conquerable. Remind yourself every day that you make thousands of choices between when you wake up and when you go to bed.

Those choices are yours. They're also yours to change.

BUT NO ONE I KNOW
DOES THIS STUFF

We can come up with many excuses that justify why we shouldn't ever go for it. Some of them are phantoms, shadows we conjure up that allow us to let our fear win. These are things we usually think after we lie down in bed, that pop into our heads and keep us up all night. They're paranoias, anxieties, roadblocks we must work to remove. We create them and we must defeat them.

Other excuses, though, are much more real and much more daunting. One that I identify with greatly is the simple: *No one I know does what I want to do. Maybe people like me, from families like mine, who live in places like the place I live, simply don't get to do stuff like this.*

When every example of a role model feels incredibly far away, it can make them feel almost fictional. If your dream is to be a cop, and all your uncles are cops, I bet it seems really possible for you to go live your dream. But if your dream is to be an avant-garde sculptor, and all your uncles are cops, I bet it makes your dream feel like a cartoon, an impossibility. And it might make you feel like a real dope for even thinking it.

I identify with this situation greatly. Being a comedian? Being an actor? When I was a kid, those did not feel like real possibilities to me at all. (Being a podcaster was a true impossibility, because podcasting did not exist until I was in my thirties.) I can tell you exactly how many examples of working artists I had around me growing up: zero. One of the major impediments for a lot of us who have a crazy dream is that we ourselves are the first examples of crazy dreamers we encounter. Nobody around me did anything that looked like what my gut was telling me to do.

My father worked in the pharmaceutical industry. My mom was a teacher. My mom's parents were immigrants from Ireland. Pop worked as a manager at a grocery store. Nan was a housewife. On my dad's side, my grandfather worked at Westinghouse in Newark. My grandma was a Catholic school teacher. Among my aunts and uncles are people in the insurance industry, a fireman, more teachers, a few military veterans, hairdressers, workers at the town recreation department, and caterers.

My cousins swim in the same seas. Among them there are more teachers, more firefighters, more military vets, and my cousin Steve, who studied industrial design and now does something that seems awfully high pressure that I do not quite understand but respect immensely.

It's not like the people in my nonfamilial sphere of influence did anything resembling what the fire in my gut was leading me toward either. My next-door neighbor was a fireman. The bully around the block was the son of a plumber. Two of my three best friends had dads who worked in IT. The other was the son of a postal worker.

There were a few actors with roots in West Orange, but strangely enough they all grew up to be teen idols—not quite the match for my dream. David Cassidy's grandmother lived on Elm Street and he lived with her for many years before finding stardom as part of *The Partridge Family*. Ian Ziering, star of *Beverly Hills 90210*, grew up near the border of Verona. Scott Wolf from *Party of Five* was closer to the Livingston border. I never met any of them, and if I had, I don't know if I'd have asked, "How do I do what you did?," because at the end of the day, what they did was all miraculously appear on shows that made teenaged girls lose their shit. That wasn't exactly the same quest I was on.

When you don't come from a family or neighborhood that artists come out of, it's really easy to feel like a freak for wanting to do your art. Any choice that involves rejecting the traditional to embrace an unblazed trail is terrifying. Doing it when no one you know has even attempted it feels like leaping off a cliff in the middle of a dark moonless night.

There are no words of wisdom that will make this feel easier. I never feel comfortable in a room full of fancy people. To this day, if I go to see a Broadway play, I assume every single person in their seats turns and glances at me as I enter and thinks to themselves, *Who let that Irish-Catholic trash from North Jersey in here?* Sometimes I have to go to industry events where you're supposed to schmooze and rub elbows, and all I can ever think of is that I probably wore the wrong type of clothes or said the wrong type of thing, because I did not grow up in environments like this and they drive me insane. I don't like premieres. I don't like networking. I've had to walk a few red carpets in my life, and it guarantees a panic attack. I was recently required to attend an event where I had to play tennis with potential advertisers for a television network I appear on. I don't play tennis. I always assumed that when society crumbles, tennis people and I would wind up in opposite armies in the great dystopian war that would follow. Every time someone walked by with a tray of fancy hors d'oeuvres I wanted to grab them and say, *Can I come with you to wherever you go when you're not feeding these people puff pastry? Anywhere else, please, let's go.*

While I have never found the solution for feeling comfortable in a social circumstance beyond my experience, I can offer up this small solace that will make you take pride in coming from where you come from: the reward you receive for experiencing that socially uncomfortable nightmare is that your dream will remain pure, and your pursuit of it will be the opposite of pretentious. Your roots offer no guide, but they offer a ton of integrity.

No one in my neighborhood got onstage and told jokes. Nobody memorized lines and recited them in front of cameras. To my knowledge I'm the only podcaster to come from the Down the Hill region of West Orange. My life choices were nerve-racking to my family, as they were to me. There were many times in my early years when I wished I had a confidant to bounce questions off, someone like me, someone from a place like the place where I'm from. They weren't around. I buddied up with the music kids, the theater kids, the closest people I could find, but there were no oddball performance art oversharing comedians in my sphere of influence. I had to do it my own way.

But the good news is that I know the value of what my roots *did* give me. I know how to work as hard as an immigrant who busted his ass at a grocery store. Thanks, Pop. I know how early teachers have to get up, I know how on their toes firefighters have to be. While having other artists around theoretically could have been nice, being salt of the earth showed me how to get things done, and how to sniff out and avoid fake bullshit in the process.

If there's no one in your sphere who can guide you, who can shine a light on the darkness of your dreams, take a deep breath, live in that fear, and know that the journey ahead of you will alternate between being exhilarating and the most dreadful path you ever walk. That's just part of the deal.

But never forget who you are. Never forget where you come from. Think of the people who came before you who never had the chance to chase their dreams, because they were too busy living a real life. Make art that reflects them. Make art that they'd like. Make art that would make them proud. Embrace their values and trust the side-eye they cast at the fancy people. Go for it as hard as they had to in their nondreamer lives. Be the first to emerge on the other side. Remain true to them when you do.

The next kid from your neighborhood will now have you to look to, so do it the right way.

BYE BYE BIRDIE

How do you know when a dream is worth the sacrifice? In my experience, it's when it shows up in your life and leaves you with no choice but to pursue it.

From a young age, I knew that I wanted to make people laugh. When I was seven years old I'd climb onto the coffee table and impersonate comedians I saw on TV to make my mom giggle. Making my brother laugh felt like a major accomplishment. It still does. I was never the best at sports, the most confident in life, or particularly great at anything—but when I could make the other kids laugh, I always felt strong and safe.

Still, I didn't know that was a thing one could really *do*, so for many years it wasn't a dream of mine. It remained dormant, asleep somewhere inside me, waiting for the right moment to strike.

And when it did, it arrived amid chaos. I never expected it and barely even asked for it. I didn't sit down with a pen and pad and brainstorm until I came up with a dream. Instead, foundations shifted and crumbled, and there it was.

When I was in eighth grade, being part of a three-way telephone call was a *big deal*. Just having phone conversations with kids from school was a big step, even though nothing of particular consequence ever went down. An eighth grader on the phone with another eighth grader consisted mostly of statements like, "We are talking on the phone right now." It's not like we had much to say to each other. Conversations mostly focused on gossip and idle chitchat and a sense of awe at something as ordinary as a phone call.

Mike and Maria both lived up the hill. I was a Down the Hill kid. We'd become friendly, but the physical separation of our neighborhoods prevented us from becoming actual pals. Each day, we'd hang out at school, then they'd take a bus home to their side of town and I'd remain on mine. The three of us started talking on the phone at night, which was the big time. A three-way call with a guy *and* a girl was pretty much unheard of in the West Orange of my youth.

During one conversation, Mike said, "You should join the school play."

I said, "I don't want to be in the school play."

Maria said, "Why not?"

"Because I don't want to wear a costume and sing and dance around in front of people."

"Neither do we," Mike said. "But it's an excuse to stick around after school. We'll get to hang out more. And we can sneak out of rehearsals and go get food and stuff."

The play that year was *Bye Bye Birdie*, a musical. The one-sentence description of this show is: a guy named Conrad Birdie, who is for all intents and purposes Elvis, shows up in some small town and underage girls hope he commits a crime by sleeping with them—set to song.

I wasn't thrilled to sing and dance. I was there for the social side of things, so being in the chorus fit me A-okay. I figured I'd get to putz around with my pals, crack jokes in the back, and otherwise not be much involved in this dumb play. The chorus was simple, easy: you just stand around with dozens of other kids and pretend to sing. Let the enthusiastic kids actually belt out the notes. And let the poor saps who landed the lead roles worry about how it's really going.

Then an unexpected thing happened—I got one of those lead roles and became one of those saps. To be in the play all you had to do was get up next to the piano and sing in front of people as a formality. When I belted out my ditty, the director seemed a little surprised at my singing ability. To everyone's shock, including my own, I was able to carry a tune at an audible level, which was more than most of my junior high compatriots could offer.

When the parts were announced, I was cast as Randolph, the little brother of the family at the core of the show. It was about as small an actual part as one could get. But it was a part, and I got it. It was intimidating . . . but secretly I was thrilled.

When I got home from school, I told my mom. "Wait. What?"

She was as confused as I was.

"Yeah, I don't know either," I said.

"Well, I'm proud of you!" she answered. I hadn't anticipated that. Her enthusiasm really got my gears turning.

Turns out, I thought, *that if you try at things you can get recognized and praised for it. Hmm . . .*

Mike and Maria stuck to the chorus, but I took my role seriously. It made sense that I was playing the little brother. I was in eighth grade but most people thought I was still in fourth. Late bloomer doesn't begin to describe where I was at. Everyone was starting to grow, get acne, wispy dirtbag mustaches, and all the things you're supposed to get in eighth grade. But I was staying still. Getting the part of Randolph was the first time my prepubescent look was ever an asset. Determined to make this work, I memorized my part within two days. I knew every line, backward and forward. I then memorized the lines that came immediately before and after mine. Because I didn't want to miss a cue, knowing every line preceding mine was key. And because I wanted to set up the next preteen thespian to really nail the necessary emotion, knowing the line after mine also seemed like a good idea. Then I figured—*You know what? I might as well memorize in their entirety all the scenes I'm in. That way I can track the intention of the whole thing start to finish and make sure I'm a really well-oiled cog in this machine.*

I got that down within a few weeks. This was furious memorization. Any time I messed up, I was mad at myself for throwing off the rhythm. But I also knew any time another actor messed up, even in the most innocuous ways. *You said "I" instead of "We,"* I'd think to myself. Just little blips on the radar. I wouldn't get huffy or judge other people for this. *Not everyone is putting in the time I am,* I'd think. *Not everyone is as dedicated to the craft of acting as me.* Or if I thought they were talented, I'd cut them slack. *Maybe they're shaking things up, keeping it fresh for themselves. Should I try that? No, I think I'll stick to nailing this shit.*

When I had memorized every scene I was in—there were only a few—I figured, *You know what? I really want to hit the ground running with my scenes. I should memorize all the scenes that happen right before scenes I'm in, even though I'm not in those scenes.* That took another week of studying the script. When I had those scenes down, I thought, *If I REALLY want to nail this part of "little brother who participates in roughly two songs," I should just bite the bullet and memorize this entire play.*

So I did. I knew every single line of the whole damn thing. All the dialogue, the lyrics to every song, even every single stage direction. I'd never worked this hard at anything in my life. I was always a smart kid and got reasonably good grades, but I expended most of my mental energy on memorizing obscure facts about Marvel

comic book characters or the lineage of different professional
wrestling championship belts. This was the first thing I poured
myself into without reservation that was even remotely connected
to school.

Other kids in the show quickly figured out that I knew every
line. Someone would forget their words and the director would
flip through his script looking for the right line. Before he could
find the page, I had already said it. I wasn't trying to show off; I
was trying to help. People in scenes would forget lines and look at
me—I'd whisper it and help them out before anyone noticed.

Admittedly, this was a bit psychopathic and reflective of some
OCD issues that would spring up later in life, but it was also pretty
useful.

Conrad Birdie was played by Danny Tobia, the coolest kid in
school, the same kid who'd kindly stepped in and salvaged my first
ever dance with a girl a couple of years earlier. Danny had a mystique that no preteen should be able to attain. He'd always had it. In
fourth grade, we heard that this kid Danny was moving across town
and would be coming to our classroom, and legend held that he
was *cool as shit*. At that age, crosstown rumors about children's per-
sonalities don't erupt too often. We awaited his arrival with bated
breath. And when he showed up, the rumors were true. This kid had
swagger. He was nine, but when he walked into a room he took alpha
male status. Teachers would shut up when he spoke. In the halls,
in between classes, older kids got out of his way. Even the principal
seemed intimidated by him. The kid knew how to run shit.

There was no one else in our school who could dream of playing Conrad Birdie. My guess is that before they even picked the
show, the director must have gone to Danny Tobia for a sit-down.

"Mr. Gitter, how can I help you today?"

"Danny, thanks for taking the time. I know you're a very busy
man."

"Come now, Mr. Gitter—"

"Please, Danny, call me Jay."

"Jay—a man of your skills and abilities, someone who gives back to the community as much as yourself. I always make time for such people."

"Danny, that means the world. I come to you with a request that would mean so much to this town. I want to put on a play."

"A play?"

"A show. A musical. I want to make the whole town of West Orange, New Jersey, sing. I want people to feel good about themselves. To get lost in the music. To have one night—*one stinkin' night!*—where they can forget all their problems."

"And how can I be of service?"

"Danny. Would you do me the great honor of playing Conrad Birdie? He's the embodiment of cool and only you can possibly pull this off."

"Normally I like to stay out of the spotlight. But for you, Jay? I'll make an exception."

Danny Tobia *was* Conrad Birdie. Before we even knew about this play, his life had mirrored it. Rumors of a cool kid showing up, people fawning over him when he finally got there—he didn't even have to act; he just had to reenact the actual path he'd blazed back in fourth grade. He was great onstage, too. He'd walk into the spotlight, mumble his lines, and the girls would flip out. Not because it was scripted that they had to, but because that's the effect he had on his female classmates. He was effortless. He was the show.

And then out of nowhere, he quit.

My hunch is that as we got closer to showtime, it was dawning on Danny more and more that he actually had to stand up in front of the entire town and do this. And Mr. Gitter started giving Danny notes. Danny didn't like getting notes. There wasn't any aspect of Danny's world in which he was used to being critiqued in front of his peers, certainly not by the likes of Mr. Gitter. And one day, he'd had enough.

Mr. Gitter was snipping at him about some missed choreography, and Danny just mumbled, "You know what? Fuck this."

The room went silent.

"Excuse me?" Mr. Gitter asked.

"I don't wanna do this," Danny said. Then he turned around and walked out of the auditorium. Mr. Gitter watched him go, then stomped back into his office. The girls cried. No one was sure what to do. Later that night, on our three-way call, Mike, Maria, and I agreed that this was some of the juiciest drama of our young lives.

The play was only a few weeks out, so we had no idea if the show was still on. I was one of the first at practice the next day, because right out of the gate I had latched on to the old acting adage of "early is on time, on time is late, late is unacceptable." When I walked in, a few of the lead actors were pleading with Mr. Gitter, who sat on the edge of the stage looking frazzled and grumpy.

"There he is," my friend Kristy said. "Try it. I swear, it's true."

"What's going on?" I asked.

"Kristy is claiming that you have the entire show memorized."

I thought I was being scolded.

"Uh . . ."

"She's saying it's not just your part. She's saying you have every role memorized. She's saying you have Conrad Birdie memorized."

I glanced at Kristy. Why was she trying to get me in trouble?

"She's saying you could play Conrad Birdie. That maybe, just maybe, we won't have to cancel this show. Is that true?"

Did not compute. Still. But I told the truth.

"I, uh . . . I have it memorized."

He opened the script to a random page and spat out a line. I didn't hesitate. I spat out Conrad's response. Another random line. I nailed that one too. His eyebrow raised. He walked to the piano and, without a word, started playing "Honestly Sincere." Without missing a beat, I sang on time and in key and nailed every word.

"You gotta be kidding me," Mr. Gitter said.

And just like that, I was Conrad Birdie. I was as far away from Conrad Birdie as a kid could be. But all of a sudden, I was the embodiment of cool: I was Conrad Birdie.

After rehearsal, Mr. Gitter pulled me aside. Looking me dead in the eye, he told me, "You're not cool. Not cool at all."

Not the most appropriate thing to say to a kid.

"But Conrad Birdie is *cool*," he continued. "So even though you're not cool, your character is cool. Be an actor, goddammit! You gotta be cool!"

I did my best to get cool, but there was no way around the way I looked. I had doe eyes and soft cheeks and a high-pitched voice. I was inches shorter than the next kid and a clear foot shorter than a lot of the girls who were fawning over me onstage. It didn't help that I had a severe bowl haircut. I had the vibe of a young k.d. lang if she wore her hair down and had much softer features.

I worked my ass off at this new part. I could feel the other kids in the cast shifting from terror that my recasting would be a horrible disaster to respect at the way I was going after it. One day, about a week after I was handed my new role, rehearsal started late because Mr. Gitter was in his office talking with Danny Tobia. Cooler heads had prevailed. Much like the Mafia impresarios he so closely resembled, Danny took a breath and realized commitments should be honored and that your word was your bond. He offered to come back to the show. It made total sense and I was ready to put on my coonskin cap to play Randolph again. But Mr. Gitter decided he was the only diva allowed in this production and told Danny he could sit out. It was shocking. The lunchroom gossip was abuzz. I had actually been *chosen* over Danny.

"It's not about you," Danny told me in science class. "It's me versus Gitter. His day of reckoning will come. In the meantime, make me proud. You go out and get them."

I had the blessing of the don, but with less than three weeks of rehearsal left to go, I was under a lot of stress.

I did have one thing going for me: two insane costumes. A glittery gold-jacket-and-pants combo, John Lennon–style sunglasses, which my blond bangs hung over, and rounding out the strange garb a scarf. It was a little Liberace, a little "1950s vision of a space-age future."

Then, the killer—my best friend Anthony's mom went above and beyond. She was the first supporter of my artistic dreams. She got behind this Conrad Birdie thing hard. And lucky for me, she was crafty.

"Go buy a white denim jacket," she told me. "Make sure it fits snug. I'll do the rest."

I did as I was told. I dropped off a plain white jacket at her house. It was simple, no frills. This jacket, it turned out, was a caterpillar. And at the end of the week Anthony's mom gave me back a butterfly: a power jacket with giant red lips bedazzled on the back below the embroidered words *CONRAD BIRDIE*. In the early '90s, few tools were as powerful as a BEDAZZLER. I may not have felt like Conrad Birdie, but my outfits certainly did.

Opening night came. People freaked out. Kids who had dreams of acting experienced stage fright for the first time. As the prospect of public humiliation set in, girls were crying, guys who were normally full of wisecracks and bravado silently slinked around with eyes full of fear. The adults were hardly better. Random parents who volunteered to help with makeup shouted across the room at no one in particular. Mr. Gitter walked past me and threw a script into the air for no reason. Everyone was tight and on edge.

But strangely, I was calm. I was an anxious kid my whole life, but for some reason I couldn't have felt more laid-back. I was about to walk onto a stage in front of a couple hundred kids I went to school with, as well as their siblings and their parents, all while wearing a shiny gold outfit made of some kind of stretchy material. (This outfit was bad. If Freddie Mercury was like "Hey, David Bowie, I'm gonna come up with something even you'll be embarrassed walking around in," this would have been it.) But I was good to go.

My entrance was hyped up by every character in the early half of the show. Everything in the first act leads up to the entrance of Conrad Birdie . . . the *coolest motherfucker anyone has ever seen*. Scene after scene, it's people preparing for Conrad. Waxing poetic about the coolness of Conrad. Bracing themselves . . . for Conrad.

The moment of the big entrance arrived. The curtain opened.

And *I* walked out.

At first there was stunned silence. Then a handful of the crowd giggled. Laughter. Not cheers. Not being impressed by how cool Conrad Birdie was. The giggles spread, then turned into belly laughs. Gut ones, instinctive ones. People doubled over. Genuine laughs, to this day some of the hardest I've ever caused.

For forty minutes, all the audience heard were people talking about the coolest person on planet Earth arriving, and when the moment came a prepubescent boy who looked vaguely like a '90s-era lesbian songwriter strode onto the stage.

I didn't blink. I loved it. *I get it*, I thought. *I get why this is funny*. Instincts I didn't know I had kicked to life. It was like an equation: *A guy who looks like me is not supposed to get this reaction from girls. The more I can just be like me, the more the crowd will laugh. I can work with this. I can make this get even bigger.*

I have them, I thought. *I have them right where I want them.*

I milked it hard. I'm not saying I put in some tour-de-force performance. I was an eighth grader onstage for the first time. But I loved going out there. Any line where I had to hit on a girl got roars. My songs were met with cheers. Crowds at middle-school shows are prone to support and enthusiasm, so they're always going to be nice, but I felt the emotions of the crowd—they were enjoying me, rooting for me. Something unique was happening.

Every time I stepped offstage, I wanted back out there. I'd turn and watch the scenes I wasn't in, swaying back and forth, hopping on the balls of my feet like a boxer waiting for the fight to start. When my cue came, I had to restrain myself from sprinting back out onstage. All I wanted was to make people laugh again. It came from my guts, an animal impulse. I wanted more. I'd spent a whole life praying people *wouldn't* laugh at me. Now I wanted a room full of kids, parents, teachers, anyone who passed by in the hallway and happened to glimpse into that beat-up auditorium—I wanted them all to laugh at me.

When the show was over, we bowed and the curtains closed. There was panic. Kids ran up to each other and hugged, cried, consoled each other over mess-ups. Adults barked commands at the stage crew, musicians sprinted through with music stands. It was mayhem.

And I was in the middle of it. The chaos felt like a warm blanket. A bubble of space formed around me. It was strange and felt supernatural. To this day I have no idea why, but I was in the center of the stage and despite the crazy amount of activity surrounding me, no one came within ten feet of me in any direction. It was like a force field protected me. And in that ten feet, I spun, then jumped, then spun some more, thinking to myself—

This is it. This is it, this is it, this is it.

A show had fallen apart. I tumbled downhill as it did and somehow wound up being the core of it. Chaos shook this whole thing down like an earthquake, and when it was over I was smart enough to see my path sitting there in front of me and was brave enough to go for it.

I never found my dream. It found me.

What I'm telling you is that you will know it is time to dedicate a significant portion of your time, energy, and focus to a project when you can't escape it. When you experience something that leads to inspiration and motivation, you will likely find that the motivation doesn't leave you. Like a cloud, it sits and hangs there, hovering over you.

Dreams can fester and grow into unexorcized demons. If you can let them go, let them go. There's absolutely no need to live your life chasing something you don't feel bound to. But when a dream sits and grows and doesn't go away, that's the one you must attack and figure out. These are the dreams that you feel in such true fashion that it's worth failing hard to find out if something's actually there.

At the end of the day, your dream will find you as much as you will find it. When you and your dream finally link up, be like Conrad Birdie: honestly sincere. Make them feel it too.

WHY THIS? WHY HERE? WHY NOW?

At the beginning of any new creative venture, I like to drill myself on three simple questions:

Why this? Why here? Why now?

All three of these questions are simple, to the point, and intended to help me remain focused on my goals.

If my answers to these questions feel muddled or—worse—don't come, I know that I need to flesh out my ideas more. If I can't explain why a thing is necessary in this time and place as its creator, I assume anyone asked to consume it will be confused as well. But if I can answer those three questions in a straightforward, simple, and confident fashion, I know there's something at least worth bringing to fruition. Like all endeavors, odds are that it will fail, but asking myself these three questions gives me permission to at least try.

My podcast, *Beautiful/Anonymous*, presents a good example. It's a simple premise: I tweet out a phone number. I put one caller on the line and talk to that person for an hour. They never tell me their name. I'm not allowed to hang up.

When I first pitched this, the head honchos at the Earwolf podcasting network were hesitant. They weren't sure anyone would be into it. To be fair, talking to a random person for an hour is a bit of an odd idea. But I stuck to my guns, because before pitching the podcast, I asked my three questions, and I knew I could trust my answers.

Why this? Because there are a ton of podcasts that put celebrities on a pedestal, but not so many that allow regular people the opportunity to climb atop one. And because as a longtime improvisor, I trust my abilities to turn these conversations into something interesting. On top of that, everyone has a phone on them at all times these days. They need one tool to participate, and they definitely have it. It's in their pocket right now. Realistically, it's probably already in their hand right now. If I tweet them a phone number to call to get in on the game, they're holding the thing in their hand that lets them get started.

Why here? Because this podcasting thing is booming, and because I've sensed this undiscovered territory within it. Because podcasting allows for free-form conversations, for rambling. Unlike television, or the written word, it doesn't need to be over-edited or controlled. People who like podcasts tend to like things that are raw, unedited, and even meandering more than they like tightly scripted projects. This idea, by its definition, can't be predicted. I might get a real motormouth on the phone, I might get the most boring person on planet Earth. In that sense it's like playing the lottery, in a way that the internet consumer is built to enjoy. On a basic level, the internet is still open enough to accommodate this idea.

Why now? Because we live in an age of social media where people use platforms to tell their own stories. But they have to do that 140 characters at a time, or through status updates or by uploading photos. There's a culture of oversharing right now, but I realized there were few long-form versions of that. If I take the culture of social media sharing and combine that with the popularity of interview podcasts, this could hit. Now is the time to strike.

Those three answers were clear. Any time we brainstormed how to beef up the idea, I always kept them in the back of my mind, using them as the podcast's core principles and goals. If I could find a way to present this idea that would accomplish those goals in as efficient a way as possible, it was worth going for.

Luckily, it worked. The initial skepticism was unnecessary. Right out of the gate, people embraced the idea. Turns out, people in 2016 liked to talk about themselves. *Beautiful/Anonymous* was featured on *This American Life* and each episode is downloaded more than one hundred thousand times. It's become a surprise success and one of the backbones of my entire career. It was the quickest, simplest success I've ever had as an artist.

And the path to that success was paved with the guidance of three simple questions. Ask them whenever you're considering your own impending life alterations. If you can answer them simply and right away, a clear path is presenting itself to you. You need to find strength in that and at least give yourself permission to try.

PFIZER WINTER

What's the hardest you've ever worked? What's the hardest you've ever seen someone else work? Living in a society that allows us to chase dreams at all is a luxury. But what about the real work of people just paying their rent? Think of the hardest workers you know, and think of them often. They will inspire you far more often than you realize and remind you of the values you need to survive when your path isn't as easy as the next person's.

Success is never found. Nor is it effortless. It's not something you trip over walking down the street. It doesn't fall from the sky and land in front of your feet. Your dreams might sucker punch you in the face, but success? That has to be cultivated. Success is the result of many things coming together all at once. Inspiration, skill, timing, luck, and so many more. And because all these elements are volatile and unpredictable, the only quality you can control is hard work.

You can't force luck. You can't make connections with power brokers exist out of thin air. What you can do is spend more time in the trenches than the person next to you. You can wake up an hour earlier than you're used to so you have time to pour yourself into your dream. You can skip the night out drinking with your college buddies if you're working on a deadline. You can sacrifice. You can do some heavy lifting in service to yourself. You can work.

Hard work is the fuel that powers everything, the gas that makes the engine run. It's what keeps your dream up and running long enough for all those other factors to fall into place. If you aren't working hard, luck will never come anyway. Luck, it turns out, is reserved for the people willing to break their backs. Overnight successes, it turns out, are carried by calloused hands.

Before you take the first step toward your dream, whatever it may be, take a deep breath and spend a few moments thinking about the hardest you've ever worked. Know that you've got to outwork that. However hard you've gone at completing a job, realizing a dream requires even more effort. You are claiming ownership of your dream, which means you're going to be exhausted physically, mentally, emotionally, and financially. Don't even stop at your own hard work. Think of the greatest examples of hard work you've ever seen. What's the closest you've stood next to true back-breaking work? Who are the people you know who had to hustle for real? Can you match them, can you keep up? Can you, as a person pursuing something born of yourself, honor the hard work they put in and follow the industrious example they set?

Working-class dreamers are a rare breed of people who know the intrinsic value of effort and honesty. Never forget that living your dream doesn't mean walking away from your working-class ethic. In fact, those ideals are the first step toward getting there.

My father worked in the pharmaceutical industry, and in traditional fashion he started at the bottom and worked his way up. At no point in my life have I ever been quite sure of what his job actually entailed. When I was very young, he worked at a company called Graver. Their website says the company deals with "filtration, adsorption, and ion exchange products." I can't even hazard a guess as to what that means. (I thought *adsorption* was a typo until I ran it through spell-check.) What I do know is that during that stretch my father wore a blue work shirt and, at the end of his workday, smelled vaguely of fish.

He spent much of his career working at Pfizer, and I'll ask that you withhold judgment on that. I get it. When you type "Is Pfizer" into a Google search bar, it autofills to read "Is Pfizer evil?" My father was not working there when the company agreed to pay the largest health-care fraud settlement in United States history, and even when he was there he worked on more of their innocuous products. Visine, for example.

Visine are eye drops all Americans learn about roughly around the age of thirteen, which is when your early adopter classmates start smoking weed. "Get the red out" is a pretty effective slogan, and teenage potheads have been embracing the message for years. We forget about products like this, that they come from some-where.

I can vouch personally for the fact that at least in the late 1990s, a lot of Visine came from a since-shuttered Pfizer plant in Parsippany, New Jersey. I know this because my father forced me to work there and it remains the most stunning glimpse into what real work looks like that I have ever experienced.

To this day, my father works harder than anyone else I know. The guy got a doctorate in environmental science *for fun*. He did that a year or two before he retired. It wasn't for career advance-ment. He just likes to learn more about a subject he loves. The only reason I would even enter an academic environment at this stage in my life would be to give a stirring '80s movie-style moti-vational speech urging the kids to bust out and do their own thing. (I'd enter this situation thinking it was going to be the beginning of some sort of campuswide teenaged rebellion that viewed me as an older but still cool countercultural figurehead.

In reality, the kids who paid attention would be vaguely embarrassed for me, while the rest of their classmates would be killing time on Snapchat.)

I didn't get a job at Pfizer so much as my dad told me I had a job at Pfizer. And it wasn't "You have this job unless you can find something more in your wheelhouse." It was "Winter break is coming up. You're working at Pfizer." I was bummed. This was the winter of 1999, a few weeks before the calendar flipped to 2000. Everyone was talking about Y2K. Not only was I a college sophomore who wanted to party, I'm also a big fan of potential dystopian postapocalyptic worlds. I didn't want to miss out.

The first morning of my winter job, the alarm went off. My father was already awake. I threw on a pair of sweatpants and a hoodie and, wiping sleep from my eyes, wandered outside to start my car. I cranked the defrosters to their maximum, then scurried back inside to take a hot shower. "Start the car before you shower" work is a specific kind of hard work. You're waking up before the sun starts to thaw the ice. You've learned the natural order of things: start the car, then take a shower. If you shower first, your hair will freeze at the ends as soon as you step outdoors. Also, the car gets you to the factory so it is right now the more important piece of the puzzle than you are. Better to start the more important process and get the vehicle warm and ready. You and your car are both just cogs in the machine when it comes to jobs like this.

My father and I didn't drive to work together, because he always left earlier than me, and there was no predicting when his day would end. Each morning, I got out of the shower, dried off my hair, jumped into my warmed-up car, and slogged my way up Route 46 to Route 80, passing on my way a Sheraton shaped like a castle, which was perched high up on a hill right before Pfizer's Parsippany facility, an antiseptic world that couldn't have been less regal.

I was one of a handful of children of workers on the factory floor. All of us were installed in pretty cushy jobs, the kind of work hungover college kids could handle. I was placed on the "women's line." Now, look, I don't agree with the gender politics of calling an easy job a "woman's" job, and when I've told this story in the past, people have jumped on me for it. Please keep in mind that on a factory floor, people don't give as much of a fuck about gender politics. If there is a section of the assembly line where all the workers are women who are too old to work other jobs, then the shorthand for that is "the women's line." Trust me, everyone is okay with it, including the women, who, like Rosie the Riveter before them, took a special pride in the designation. These hair-netted older ladies had served their time well and were now coasting to retirement. Their hands were calloused from whatever darker, more dangerous corners of this factory they worked in for decades prior to their final assignment on the women's line. Their backs were bent. After lifting and pushing and pulling and grinding away for years, Pfizer rewarded them with this easy gig, a respected job reserved for older women who knew what they were doing—and the pampered sons of managers and executives in between semesters the women watched over to make sure we didn't mess up. It wasn't a coincidence that there hadn't been a work stoppage injury on the women's line in decades.

My job was simple. I monitored a part of a conveyor belt that turns all the Visine bottles to face in the same direction. Visine bottles entered a sorting machine jumbled, at weird angles. They exited the other side of the machine in a straight line, facing forward. All I had to do was watch this hunk of metal to make sure fallen Visine bottles didn't clog up either opening, which would have backed up the conveyor belt—an unacceptable and costly outcome, I was warned time and time again. When a bottle of Visine inevitably tipped over, I used a flat green stick to wiggle free the errant bottle, then went back to standing still in front of the once again functioning machine.

It was an easy job, and a very boring job. Luckily, the women of the women's line were a group of Chatty Cathys. All they *ever* wanted to talk about was the apocalypse. And I was down.

It makes total sense to me that *The Walking Dead* is as popular as it is, because as someone who grew up right on the cusp of working and middle class, I can tell you that blue-collar workers in America love nothing more than the apocalypse. If they could, they would talk about it all day. Do you know your emergency apocalypse escape plan? Everyone I grew up with had one. Working-class people who live near bodies of water *definitely* own inflatable rafts. Crovel. Do you know what that is? Probably not. People who work assembly lines own one.

The guy who oversaw the women's line was a nice man named Carlos. He respected my dad a lot. The alpha of the environment, though, was a feisty lady named Jan, who told it like it was, even if telling it like it was didn't involve being factually correct or even logical. Much of the day on the women's line was spent with Jan saying things out loud in emphatic and declarative fashion and the women on the line nodding in agreement, while I just listened, amazed and more than a little afraid.

"The Clintons are definitely really Rothschilds. And they killed that guy Vince."

"Mm-hmm." "Mm-hmm." "Yup."

"There's a shadow government and everyone knows it. There's a secret second president and vice president and Supreme Court. And somebody knows where the Holy Grail is, they have to."

"Damn right." "Mm-hmm."

"The Jersey Devil is real."

The conversation would build like this until Carlos stepped in to say it was time to focus back on the work. "Jan, let's focus up, huh?"

"Sure, Carlos."

Beat. Carlos walks away.

"Fuckin' Carlos."

There are few things I enjoy more than talking about Free-masonry with middle-aged women. Still, there are only so many hours you can spend arguing about the chupacabra before even the liveliest points become background noise.

Fortunately, the Y2K winter gave us an exciting topical level of apocalypse to constantly gab about. I'm not sure what the information pipelines were for the ladies of the line, but they had the inside scoop on a lot of stuff I wasn't hearing about elsewhere.

For anyone too young to remember, the big rumor in the winter of 1999 was that computers weren't programmed to move beyond the 1900s and that they were going to go apeshit once the calendar turned to the year 2000. There were real hyped-up news stories about how no one knew how this was going to affect computer-reliant industries, small industries you've probably heard of like banking or the government or nuclear reactors. For a few weeks before New Year's, everyone I knew took a "let's quietly make jokes about this and assume it's not going to be that bad" tone about the impending doom.

Not the line ladies. They were convinced that when the clock struck midnight and the year 2000 was upon us, mayhem was going to redefine every moment of our lives. Some said the computers were going to gain sentience and, at long last, just as James Cameron prophesized, we'd be in a Terminator-esque standoff with them. Others thought computers would cease to function forever, and we'd have to return to a predigital world where we, ya know, read by candlelight and talked to each other and churned butter and looked at maps from time to time.

The women's line ladies spoke very freely in front of me. From conspiracies and the quality of the lunch room's food to Christmas presents they were getting their kids and which of the higher-ups at the company were assholes. (Any time this topic was breached Jan would look me in the eye and say, "Your dad's a good man." I'd give a nod to let them know I understand that snitches get stitches, and they'd then shit all over my dad's peers in front of me.) Even coded allusions to the ladies' sex lives were fair game.

The only thing I couldn't get them to talk about was New Year's Eve.

No matter how hard I tried, I couldn't get anyone on that line to answer the simplest question—"What are your plans for New Year's?" Evasive mumbling, nonresponses, outright pretending I hadn't even asked.

A couple of weeks into my employment, I was sitting by myself in the cafeteria when Jan beckoned me to come sit at a table with her and some of my other women's line compatriots.

"Look," she told me. "There's something we haven't told you."

The other women shifted and exchanged cautious looks.

"New Year's Eve, a bunch of us have all put in on a cabin," Jan told me. "We're gonna hide out there so that when shit goes down we're in it together and we'll live off the land."

"Oh," I said. "That seems like a smart plan."

"It is," Jan told me. "You're a good kid so I didn't want to hide it from you. But also, there's no more room in the cabin. You can't come. A lot of people want in who can't fit. They're mad."

"I get it," I said.

"Yeah." She sighed. "I mean, it's like they think we're leaving them to die. It's not that. They just have to survive on their own."

"I'm sure they'll be fine," I said.

She raised her eyebrow. "We'll see. There's four of us, and our husbands. We got canned food, water, and board games. And guns."

"Sounds like that'll be the safest cabin in Jersey."

"Fuck Jersey, it's in Maine," she said. "We want to be close to the border."

New Year's came and went. I partied at my buddy Mike's house in New Brunswick, the perfect place to ring in the millennium.

Around 11:25 I felt a hand on my shoulder. Mike, whom I have known since the age of thirteen, gave me a nod and I followed him into his room.

"If shit goes down, I'm surviving. There's a blue truck parked halfway down the block," he said. "Meet me there. It fits five of us. I have the quickest route to the Appalachian Trail mapped out. We get there, we head south. I have a tent and a gun. You good?"

"I'm good."

Midnight approached and the party was fun, but we all held our breath as the clock counted down. Right before midnight, I made eye contact with Mike and knew I'd be fine, no matter what happened, apocalypse or not. He and I were from the same neighborhood. Though we were trying to rise above it, as each generation has to, we still shared the values of our parents' time. And that meant knowing we could scrap it out, that we'd be the first to survive, that we had our plan. I am what I am. I am where I come from. I never can change that. Nor do I want to.

Since the computer apocalypse never came, we all celebrated even harder than we normally would have at a college New Year's party. I got cross-eyed drunk, danced in a sink, and poured an entire bottle of champagne over my head. (In the moment, I thought this was *very* cool, but when I was later shown a photograph of this behavior it directly contributed to my decision to quit drinking.)

I returned to the line in the new year, ready to finish out my final few weeks before the spring semester started up. Unfortunately, my holiday partying caught up with me a bit. I was a college kid, already not used to getting up at 5:30 a.m., let alone after long nights of drinking. So my first day back on the floor after a few days off and a few careless nights, I was practicing the time-honored art of sleeping while standing up. Holding my green stick, drifting off to the soothing sounds of industrial machinery, I stood at my station dreaming of Visine bottles.

I felt a hand on my shoulder. It was Carlos.

"Your dad's a good guy, dude," he told me. "But you gotta at least be awake."

Fair point, I thought to myself, wondering why the ladies of the women's line regarded Carlos as such an asshole. He seemed fine to me. I let out a yawn.

Then the next thing I remember a horn was blaring. It's an alarm. People are yelling, pointing at me. Ladies at the far end of the room waved their hands, motioning wildly at my station. I had fallen asleep. This much was clear, but I didn't know what everyone was worked up about. I looked down. A critical mass of Visine bottles gummed up the works. The machine I stood in front of was supposed to send each bottle of Visine through a small slot, turning it in the right direction for the label to be placed on. Because of my negligence, about a dozen bottles were now all caught in that slot trying to make it through at the same time. The bottles were getting crushed, exploding Get-the-Red-Out liquid everywhere. Visine dripped off the conveyor belt and the machine itself, which was now also making a sickening wheezing grinding sound. In my sleepy confusion I simply stared at this scenario instead of stopping it. More bottles of Visine headed into the maelstrom. Some got pulled into the fray, adding to the mess. Dozens of other bottles simply fell off the sides of the conveyor belt, clattering all over the floor.

If I could clear the path to that slot, everything would be fine. All I had to do was shove my green stick into the growing blob of Visine bottles.

Instead, I reached down into the machine with my left hand, keeping the stick at my side. Immediately my hand got sucked into the sorting machine's gears, which is when I quickly learned why the stick is the tool of this trade. The machine made a sound like someone had dropped an uncooked flank steak onto a circular saw, and I was yanked forward. I screamed. A two-inch gash cut across my pinkie. Blood splattered the conveyor belt.

I could see women's mouths moving as they shouted in my direction. Between the screech of the machinery and the pain in my hand, I couldn't make out what they were saying. Carlos ran into the room, lifted a glass case on the wall, and pushed the button inside. Everything stopped. This room, which was never quiet, fell deafeningly silent. I breathed heavily and clutched my left pinkie in my right hand, watching blood drip out as it spread over my palm. I was sent to the factory's nurse, who took one look at my sliced finger and said it was out of her depth. She sent me to a hospital, where my pinkie was laced with stitches. This was the first work stoppage injury on the women's line in well over a decade.

For months, my dad had to live it down. "Was it your son that got cut up on the *women's line*?"

I learned my lesson. And not just the one about "Don't stick your hand into industrial machinery." A much more important one.

I'd often wondered why my dad made me take that job. Now that I am who I am, I think his reason is pretty simple. He sensed he had a son who was about to walk his own path. He didn't know where I was heading—nobody did—but he knew it wasn't going to be traditional, corporate, shirt-and-tie stuff. Probably before I did, my dad realized I was a dreamer, and he wanted to make sure that before I walked off the grid I saw real work, hard work, face-to-face. He needed me to see the bent backs, the gnarled knuckles, the tough talk of those women. He needed me to get to work before the sun came up. He needed me to spill a few drops of my own blood over a thankless machine.

People like me and you—people who aren't afraid to put in the work—don't get to skip to the end. We don't get to leave our life behind us and land smack-dab in money or fame or validation. All we get to do is put in the work. Success is about scrapping it out. It's about removing your safety net and dedicating time you don't really have toward putting all your effort into something unlikely. People like us have to put our mental, physical, and financial well-being on the line, gratefully, day after day, until by some miracle we figure out how to bleed for something we believe in more powerfully than an assembly line.

Success always starts with rising before the sun. With keeping the car running and knowing that your hair will freeze. It starts with scraping ice off your windshield. It starts with the privilege of backbreaking work.

Dreamers, people like me and you, shouldn't want it any other way.

WHEN SHOULD I QUIT?

There's no shame in quitting! I'm all for it.

As long as you ride this thing out to the edge of your own comfort zone, you're allowed to walk away. When you've answered the questions nipping at your soul, you can let out a sigh and move on with your life. You'll be less tortured. I'm jealous.

One of the big questions about quitting is when to quit. How do you know when it's the right time to call it a day and walk away?

I think you have exactly two options: never, or at this exact moment.

If the question of quitting pops into your head, decide right then—yes or no. If the answer is yes, it means you've put out the fire. If the answer is no, put your head down and get back to work.

When you get back to work, though, forget that quitting was on your mind. One of the least productive mind-sets for creativity is the dangerous middle ground of half in and half out. Sitting around with vague self-imposed deadlines never helps. "I'll give it a year." You can't work that way, with an arbitrary doomsday clock you installed yourself. It's the opposite of "giving yourself no other option." It's reserving the right to explore *any* other option at some undetermined point in the future. It means you're focusing on all the possible escape hatches instead of the task at hand.

You have to work under the premise that though success might feel far away, it's possible and it's potentially imminent. Setting goals can be healthy, especially if they're used to track markers of your progress. "If x hasn't happened by this date, I'm going to reevaluate." That feels fair to me. It's firm, it's aimed at a goal, and it's set as an evaluation point that's built into your progress. That's a lot different from "I'm still figuring out if this is even for me." You shouldn't bang your head against a wall if it's not for you. It's for you. If it's not, there's no reason to put your life under the strain of attacking it. You are allowed to fail, as I always say. But you have to fail with firm intention, not because you aren't willing to give it your all.

In the world of comedy, I've met hundreds of comedians who are "feeling it out." From what I can tell, most of these people don't want to be comedians. They want to live the comedian lifestyle. They want to stay out late, drink on weeknights, sleep in. They don't want to actually put in the work it takes to complete projects, pitch them to power brokers, and see them through to the end. They haven't decided that these things are necessary for them to push every button their soul needs them to, so they never will.

I have never seen one of these people make it.

Go all in or get out of the way. Falling on your face while all in can be a zenlike experience that shows you things about your life and the state of your mind. Failing because you were too cool to try doesn't give you or the world shit.

You can't create anything good when you're giving yourself the pressure release of a vague and hazy "I dunno about this. I might quit."

If you might quit, you already have.

THE FALCON

You won't know when, or what form it will take, but a reckoning is always imminent. When it comes, you'll need to handle it, to do the dirty work, and break your back.

Right now, you want to accomplish something. It's hard. If it were easy, you wouldn't be frustrated. Odds are that the difficulties you face will not be taken care of for you. You'll have to conquer them yourself.

The ability to do dirty work on your own behalf is the difference between being entitled and being deserving.

At some point you're going to face a put-up-or-shut-up moment. Getting in the trenches is how you'll prove to yourself and all your doubters that you're willing to fall on your face on your own terms. When people doubt you, one of the only surefire ways to send them an emphatic "Shut the fuck up" is to get your own hands dirty and show them how it's done.

The greatest example of a "get in the trenches" mentality in my own life is when I took my television show to the uncharted frontier of public access television. This wasn't just a creative risk; it was a logistical nightmare. Not only did I have to make a show

I was proud of, I had to convince a gang of two dozen comedians, musicians, film kids, and assorted weirdos—all of whom helped in unpredicted ways—to keep showing up and working for free on this thing with my name on it. I wasn't pampered on public access. I needed to prove to everyone involved that I was ready to hustle to make it happen. Hustling would prove the show was worthy of its existence and demonstrate to the people willing to have my back that I wasn't wasting their time and considerable talent.

The ultimate proof that I was willing to get my hands dirty was the trunk of my car. We didn't get a storage locker at the public access studio. We weren't allowed to leave anything there week to week. All we got was the promise that the studio was ours, with about forty minutes of prep time before the show went live every Wednesday night at eleven. During those forty minutes, we had to get all the audio up and running, get the lights focused correctly, and build the set.

And that set lived, for four years, in the trunk of my car.

On any given Wednesday between 2011 and 2014, if you stood on Fifty-Ninth Street between Tenth and Eleventh Avenues, you'd see me driving my beat-up 2001 Nissan Sentra, most likely with a panicked look on my face as I desperately looked for a parking spot across the street from our studio. Because nothing involved with public access is ever easy or convenient, the block was located on the steepest hill I've yet to encounter in Manhattan. If I couldn't find a spot out front, I'd have to park at the bottom of the hill, which meant my night was going to be a little sweatier and a lot more of a pain in the ass.

I'd park the car. I'd pop the trunk. I'd remove the suitcase full of our assorted audio gear—wires, clips, and all sorts of other equipment I didn't know how to use. After setting the audio gear on the curb, I'd remove our show's backdrop, a gigantic canvas drop cloth I bought at Home Depot. I spray-painted the words *The*

Chris Gethard Show on it, and every band who ever played our show signed it. The backdrop lived in a tote bag, which I'd hang over my neck. Then I'd remove the stand the backdrop hung from, which folded into a four-foot-long tube. I'd grab any props we were using that episode. Once that meant a bag of sex toys for our dominatrix episode. Other episodes required different props, like six toy bats for our "Wiffle Bat Gang" episode, cardboard robot outfits for our "Robot Fights" episode, or giant Nerf guns we mounted on the camera for our "Camera Cannon" episode. That trunk was home to all sorts of weird shit, because invariably any time I threw away a prop we'd need to use it again. Eventually, I got tired of buying the same dildos over and over again, so I just kept my collection of sex toys and other props in the trunk of my Nissan.

Every week with the canvas bag hanging from my neck, I'd drag all that shit uphill, my arms draped over the banner's stand in a Christ-like crucified vibe, lugging behind me with one hand the suitcase of audio equipment and the bag of props with my other hand. If I were lucky, someone who worked on the show would arrive around the same time and help me. Sometimes fans who were lining up for the show would take pity on me and grab an item or two. It's a unique type of humiliation, having one of your fans carry your bag of dildos because they saw you struggling with it. But most often, getting everything into the studio was my weekly ritual of pain to endure on my own. Sweaty and out of breath, I'd arrive at the front door of the Manhattan Neighborhood Network exhausted, and if some dumbass prop fell out of a bag and cut me or I tripped on the sidewalk, bleeding, collapsing in a heap—all before performing a live show. The door guy would buzz me in and bit by bloody bit I'd drag my own TV show into the studio, where the crew would grab what they needed off my broken and battered body and get to work setting everything up.

My weekly ritual was a regular reminder that I didn't just want

this show to happen, I needed it to. No one in the television industry was interested in my show, so I did the dirty work and bloodied
up my knuckles to will it into existence.

Was it a little nuts? Yes, it was. But it was also required. Luckily,
I learned how to get my hands dirty from the best.

When I was a kid, vacation meant piling into my dad's van for a
road trip. The van was a key asset because it had a tiny TV in the
back to distract us and was spacious enough that my brother and
I could sit far enough away from each other that we wouldn't erupt
into random fistfights.

When my brother graduated from eighth grade, we embarked
on the crown jewel road trip: Disney World.

My childhood home in West Orange, New Jersey, is 1,095 miles
from the Walt Disney World Resort in Orlando, Florida. Not count-
ing stops, the trip takes sixteen hours and fourteen minutes to get
there. Which is impossible under ideal conditions, let alone when
your wife hates driving on highways and needs periodic breaks.
And *especially* when you have two kids who are constantly trying
to beat the shit out of each other in the backseat. Whenever we set
off on a long trip, I could tell my dad was putting himself someplace else. To survive any upcoming trip, he had to mentally leave
us, retreating inside his head, where it was much more peaceful
than the interior of our family's van. A zen place, somewhere deep
inside his mind, that would allow him to drive his family across
an impossible distance without winding up in a mental hospital.

The turnpike treated us kindly. Jersey was a breeze. The quick
swing along the Delaware/Pennsylvania border presented no problems. Maryland went by in a flash. But Virginia, a commonwealth,
fucked us. Bumper-to-bumper traffic. Commuters escaping Washington. Traffic stood so still a few college kids got out of their car
and tossed a Frisbee around on the highway. It was hot. We were

bored. It wasn't good. Tension was brewing, but my dad held it together. He breathed deeply. He stayed somewhere far away.

When we finally got through that mess, my dad gave it a little extra gas to make up for lost time. This made my mom very skit-tish. When my mom gets nervous in a car, she will say her signa-ture catchphrase to my dad: "Ken, watch out." If another car gets too close, it's "Ken, watch out." If a car miles ahead of us slows down: "Ken, watch out." If the wind blows too hard: "Ken, watch out." Her words of warning became such a part of our road trips they became for my father nothing more than background noise, no different from the rumble of the highway or the clicking of his turn signal.

Near the southern border of Virginia, I was sitting in the back-seat poking my brother in the neck, trying to set him off, when I hear my mom say it. "Ken, watch out." Only this time it has some unusual urgency to it. And to my surprise, my dad answers her.

"I see it."

"Ken . . . watch *out*."

"I see it. What do you want me to do?"

Alarmed, my brother and I stopped tormenting each other and looked out the front windshield.

A bird.

Not just any bird: the most intimidating bird I've ever seen. A bird of *prey*. I'm no ornithologist, nor am I certain that ornithol-ogy is the study of birds. That's how little I know about birds. But I can say for certain that this thing is not a pigeon. It's big. And it's not a hawk. I saw hawks circling high above trees around my suburban streets all the time. And while hawks are cool, they're not as big as the bird that was flying over the center of the highway, getting lower and lower, and targeting the front of our car.

We'll call it a falcon. I have no idea if falcons inhabit the East Coast. I don't even know if falcons are extinct. But just for clarity's sake, this monster bird shall heretofore be known as a falcon. No, it deserves more respect than that. This monster bird shall heretofore be known as *the* Falcon.

The Falcon was bearing down on us. It wasn't "headed in our general direction." It wasn't accidental. It had decided that my father's van was its enemy. My brother and I went silent. But my mother, she did not. Her signature slogan increased in intensity. Lost in concentration, my father only got more calm.

"Ken . . . watch out."

"I see it."

"Ken, watch OUT."

"What do you want me to do, Sal? I see it."

The Falcon got lower and faster and, in my eyes, angrier and more determined.

"Ken—"

"I know."

"Ken—"

"I see it."

The Falcon hit our van, head-on. There was a loud noise, like a pillow hitting a wall at a hundred miles an hour. Bird feathers exploded in front of the van and made scratching noises as they cascaded along the van's windows. Then . . . nothing. My father drove on. My mom said, "Oh my God, oh my God," a few times, but my father maintained the same pace. He didn't swerve. He didn't even pump the brakes. He just kept driving. My father drove, without stopping, for the next five hours, all the way through North Carolina.

Finally, just before we crossed into South Carolina, my father pulled into a rest stop, so we could eat, probably at a Hardee's or a Shonie's—one of the fast-food places we didn't have in the Northeast. (We did not stop at South of the Border, one of America's greatest roadside attractions. It's a Mexican-themed rest stop / fireworks store / condom depot / racist nightmare. Two thumbs up.) Gregg and I were thrilled. Fast food that you can't find in your region seems exciting, even though it's definitely as terrible as all the other kinds of fast food.

We exited the van. My father walked around to the front, let out a sigh, and nodded his head. He tried to stop my mother from following, but before he could she said "Oh no" and looked away. Gregg and I sprinted around the bumper, our necks craning to see what our parents were gawking at. And that's when we saw it. The Falcon. It was hanging out of the front grille at a thirty-degree angle, its back half sticking out of the hot metal like a javelin that had been tossed from afar. The Falcon had kamikaze'd our van. And, man, did it go out in a blaze of glory. I don't know if the Falcon had been riddled by depression for its whole life or if recent events had caused a sense of hopelessness, but for some reason the Falcon decided to commit suicide by attacking a speeding projectile, in this case my family's dependable plus-size van.

A full state and a half my father had driven with this thing sticking out of our vehicle. People must have thought we were insane. A big beat-up van with a bird of prey smashed across its front. This was some Mad Max shit. We were road warriors. No wonder all the other cars were getting out of our way.

Gregg said "Whoooooooa," and I yelled "Gross!" with glee, since I was a preteen boy and gross stuff rules at that age. My dad reached into his pocket, removed his wallet, and handed my mom twenty bucks.

"Get yourself and the kids whatever you guys want," he said. "Get me a number two meal. Large fries, please."

There was no emotion in his voice, no trace of fear. No recognition at all that this was anything but a normal occurrence.

My mom led us inside. We ordered our food. We sat down. We ate. Moments later my father entered the restaurant and made a beeline for the bathroom. He emerged carrying every paper towel the bathroom's dispenser had to offer and made his way back to the front of the van. With maximum curiosity, my brother and I craned our necks and watched through the window. Our vantage point wasn't perfect, but we definitely saw our father wrapping his hands in paper towels and, to our horror, yanking the Falcon from our van, piece by piece.

Wide eyes. Dropped jaws. This was epic. My dad was on cleanup duty of a real bad scene. He had no hose, no tools. What tools could even handle this? Public-restroom-grade paper towels were all that was available. He took care of it.

After ten minutes of truly gruesome work, my father reentered the fast-food joint and proceeded straight back to the john. He was in there for a long time and when he came out he reeked of industrial-grade fast-food restroom soap. There wasn't a trace of the Falcon on him. He'd rubbed his skin raw with that pink slime cleaner.

Without a word, he unwrapped his number two special and took a big bite out of it.

Maybe that's what being a dad is: not freaking out in the face of complete insanity. Because if you don't freak out, maybe the people around you won't freak out either. If you pretend that life isn't a constant stream of punches to the gut, maybe the people who depend on you won't ever get hit. Life's quicksand. My dad made me think it's stable. Life's an erupting volcano. My dad made me think it's a trip to Disney World. Life is the Falcon attacking your car. My dad made me think it's just another road trip.

My dad knew how to do his dirty work.

A reckoning always comes.

I've had my own highway adventures. In 2013, my friend Johnnie Whoa Oh threw a barbecue in his mom's backyard in Long Island.

My wife and I picked up a few pals and we all drove out there together. It was a good, laid-back day.

On the ride home, though, I hit a big-ass pothole. Right away, I felt the rumble of a deflating tire. This highway was lined with minimalls, and I veered off into the parking lot of a 7-Eleven.

"Jeez," Hallie said, "that was close."

"Yeah," I told her. "I'll change the tire. You guys go grab some stuff from the store. Get me one of those weird peanut butter and jelly things I like."

Hallie and our two friends entered the 7-Eleven. I let out a deep breath and prepared to switch my tire out for the donut—

—the donut that lived in my trunk.

Within a few minutes, that parking lot was lined with every insane prop my public access show had ever used. People in the parking lot stopped on the way to their cars and stared in confusion. I saw workers at the 7-Eleven motioning to each other so they could look.

First, I removed a sizable amount of audio and video equipment. Then, a bunch of stands. So many metal stands for different pieces of equipment. Then the canvas banner. Then a weird suitcase. And out came the props. Two four-foot-long Nerf cannons. A huge double-headed dildo. A papier-mâché head of my own likeness, with removable glasses. A bag of water-filled balls with human-shaped nipples on them. And so much more. I emptied it all, shamelessly, item by item.

It was a hot summer day, so I took off my shirt as I fished the spare and jack out of the bottom of my now empty trunk.

People stared at me, this grunting, sweaty man—who had recently lined the parking lot with sex toys and video equipment and had removed half his clothes in broad daylight. When I finally changed the tire, I put everything back into my trunk, piece by piece. Back in the trunk went the six full oversize rolls of aluminum foil, the green full-body spandex suit with attached mask, the half-deflated blow-up doll of an African American male pornography star.

My wife and friends watched the entire scene unfold from inside the air-conditioned 7-Eleven, laughing at me, drinking Slurpees. As I buttoned up my shirt, I gave them a solemn nod. Then we all got back in the car and drove home, safe and sound, able to chase our dreams for another day on our sad but beautiful terms.

There will be days when you think no one else in this world believes in you or your dreams, and you will be right. During those times, you must find a way to be your own greatest champion. Sometimes that means doing the real work yourself. Slog through the mud on your own behalf. And at the end of those days, as you stand in front of the mirror, you get to look a sweaty, messy hard worker who fights for your dreams right in the eyes.

STOP APOLOGIZING

When we decide we want to shift the standard of our life to include something new and out of the box, we tend to spend a lot of time apologizing for and justifying it. People we encounter express incredulity and we scramble to downplay the quest we're setting out on.

"YOU? You're going to learn how to SURF?" your fellow copywriter in the next cubicle over says. "I didn't even know you like the BEACH."

This immediately puts us on the defensive and, as a result, we scramble to say anything.

Just to get out of the conversation, we mumble, "I don't know, it just seems cool, I'll probably just try it once or something, whatever." No, you will not try it once. That was never the goal. The goal was to buy a wet suit, take some classes, and learn how to ride a goddamn wave.

But now that you've verbalized your doubts and publicly minimized your ultimate goal, you've tacitly given yourself permission to try it once, then quit forever.

Other people's opinions are one of the most dangerous things to our success. To remain committed to our goals and steadfast in our belief in them, we have to train ourselves and break self-defeating habits and bad practices. We have to learn to draw internal lines in the sand. The things we say about our dreams and goals get imprinted on our psyche and, because of this, we have to build a strict discipline regarding our own language in this regard. There will be enough people who doubt us along the way. We can't kowtow to their comforts and add our own voice to the chorus of doubters and haters. We say these things offhandedly in the moment, but in times of true doubt and crisis our own formerly innocuous thoughts haunt us and scare us out of pursuing the things in life we most want.

I remember a harmless conversation I once had with my brother that caused great doubts in me for years.

Weird N.J., the magazine I worked for, was expanding into a national book series. It was a big deal. But I'd also spent a few years positioning myself to attack comedy. I loved both dearly, but in my heart knew that if I didn't go all in at comedy, I'd kick myself forever.

"A lot of people are blowing up at your theater, huh?" my brother asked me. "That's cool. You gonna go at it too?"

"I dunno," I said. "*Weird N.J.* has this book thing in place, comedy's not likely. Maybe I'll just stick with writing or whatever; the comedy thing might be a bit dumb."

"Yeah," Gregg said. "That's the safe bet. That's probably the move to make."

Now, I *did not believe what I had said*. I knew that I needed to dive off the comedy cliff and see what might happen. But my brother brought up my dream. I felt insecure about it. Rather than voice my real opinion—"You know, I'm still young and I think I gotta do my best to go kick the shit out of this thing and see what happens"—I watered down my own opinion and denied it. While I could handle pointing out my own Achilles' heel, I couldn't handle the thought of someone else pointing it out for me. So what did I do? I pointed it out for them!

It's like a junior high school kid who makes fun of his own braces before the bullies can sink their teeth into it. *If I shit on myself first*, the reasoning goes, *you can't shit on me*. But you still get shitted on. Long term, it will haunt you more that it came from you. A bully you can rally against. You can find some fire in your gut and take them out. It's much more daunting to go to war with yourself.

Early in my comedy career, I'd get a weird idea every now and again that made me giggle with maniacal glee. I was doing tons of improv, and more and more storytelling—very traditional stuff. But, at the same time, I kept getting these odd impulses. It was fun to see them through to fruition.

In one of the earliest, I held a tournament where two comedians would each get five minutes to make a crowd laugh. A panel of judges sat in the front row. Whomever they deemed the winner moved on. The other person was shot, without mercy, with a paintball gun wielded by my friend Eli, a very good person who was able to turn off his morals to do this job. This show sold out. People around town talked about it. Instead of doing it again, I went back to the more basic stuff. *Don't do that again*, I told myself. *Wouldn't want to get a reputation as some oddball.*

About a year later, I staged a storytelling show where everyone was required to tell stories of pooping their pants. Instead of the traditional microphone stand or podium you might find at a storytelling show, I placed a toilet center stage. Everyone was required to pull down their pants and sit on the toilet while telling a crowd about times they shat themselves. It was also massively popular. And yet again, instead of harnessing the momentum this show offered, I let my own self-consciousness lead me right back to the traditional forms of comedy that weren't half as exciting.

I took great joy in staging a conversation at Peter McManus, a bar in Chelsea comedians love to visit. "What other comedian do you think you could beat in a fistfight?" Comedians are competitive people. These harmless conversations got analyzed in back booths with great vigor. For about a month, this became a dominant topic of conversation in my community. People created their own ranking systems. "Rob Huebel and Rob Riggle are best friends. But who would win in a fucking street fight?" "Could Bobby Moynihan take out Jason Mantzoukas?"

I was proud I'd planted the seeds for these dumb hypotheticals, which everyone in my corner of the New York comedy world seemed to obsess over. Then, a moment of inspiration struck.

A few other masochistic comedians and I rented a warehouse in Brooklyn. We set up four stanchions and connected them with police tape to make ropes for our makeshift ring. We hired a professional boxing referee. Six pairs of comedians faced off. Some of us took boxing lessons in the weeks leading up to the fights. Then, we fought.

The first fight quickly showed that this day would be taken seriously. Let's just say we all learned not to fight John Gemberling. In real life, he is a warm, inviting guy, but in the ring he has a heart of stone and a jab that can draw blood.

We filmed the day's proceedings. Everyone present at the warehouse agreed to keep the results under lock and key. We screened all six fights to a bloodthirsty sold-out crowd at the UCB Theatre. Paul Scheer took bets. I buzzed with energy. It was a thrilling night. But when I got home, I lay in my bed unable to sleep because I thought everyone was going to think all I could do well was weird stuff.

In 2009, a group of students at New York University took to my comedy. They showed up at every show I did. They sometimes wore homemade T-shirts with hand-drawn sketches of my face on them or phrases like GETH BUSY LIVING OR GETH BUSY DYING. The whole thing was surreal, and I felt like a big part of it was that they knew a low-status schlub like me shouldn't have a fan club.

But they were insistent that their affection was genuine. They started a Facebook group and one of them said, "I love Geth's storytelling show. But I'd *really* love to go to all the places in New Jersey where they take place and see them there."

It got under my skin. I felt like I was being made fun of. So I joined the group.

"I'm calling your bluff," I said. "Rent a bus. We'll do it."

To my shock, they did. We did the math and realized to make this bus pay for itself, we had to charge forty dollars a ticket. That was an exorbitant price for young comedy fans in New York City who are used to their shows being priced at five bucks.

It sold out right away. I drove people to the actual locations of some of my most strange, grim experiences and told them the tales up close and personal. I even brought a group of sixty random people into the basement of the house I grew up in, which my family had sold eleven years prior. I stood near a wall, narrating events from my childhood.

"There used to be a couch here," I informed them. "In 1997, I lost my virginity on this very spot."

"Jesus Christ, come on, man," said the owner of the house from the back of the room.

In 2009, I was feeling restless and wanted to mount some sort of new show. My sincere hope was to make something industry friendly. Something that people who have hiring power in the comedy world might see. Maybe I could get a staff writing job on one of the comedy shows that filmed in New York. *SNL. The Daily Show.* I just had to figure out how to make it clear that I could play ball by the terms of those productions. I hatched an idea: I'd always loved talk shows. Maybe I'd mount my own. I'd host it, I'd get friends to write and appear on it with me. By showing off my version of a talk show, I hoped I could put myself in a position to get a job with one someday.

The artistic director of the Upright Citizens Brigade Theatre, Anthony King, had other ideas.

"I can't stress how many people pitch me the idea of them hosting a talk show," he told me. "Everyone has that idea."

"I can see that," I said. "But I've been around for years, and I think I could make one that's really good."

"I agree," he responded. "But here's the thing I don't understand about you sometimes: Why do you want to put on a shirt and tie? Every asshole who puts on their own talk show in the comedy scene wears a suit, does a monologue with jokes about recent news, and interviews some semifamous friend they have onstage. Why would you of all people do that?"

"Because that's what talk shows are," I told him. "And I'd love to work on a talk show."

"I'm going to give you a talk show," he said. "But I'll cancel it as soon as it looks like some cookie-cutter talk show."

"I don't understand," I said.

"Dude, all your best ideas are fucking weird! No one else rents fucking buses. No one else can turn physical violence into a room of two hundred people having the most fun they've ever had. No one else can convince sixteen other comedians to voluntarily get shot by a paintball gun when they bomb. For a few years now, I haven't understood why you don't just own that shit. People love those shows. *That* has to be your talk show. All your weird ideas. I'll give you one slot a month, but it's going to be the home for that part of your brain."

"Jesus," I said. "I never thought of it that way."

This was very true. Every time I'd stage one of those weird shows,

I'd put my guard up and clamor to do some regular stuff again. I didn't want to be known as the guy with the superstrange ideas. It made me feel like everyone would see me as a total fucking weirdo.

But Anthony made me realize that *My greatest asset is that I'm a total fucking weirdo.*

People would bring the cool shows up to me after they were done. They were always enthusiastic. And I always found a way to apologize.

"Yeah, I don't know why I do that dumb shit."

"That one was fun, sure, but it's not all I do."

"I'm glad you dug that one. I've been doing a lot of stand-up lately too."

My insecurity that my ideas were too odd led to tons of apologies. I sat in that chair across from Anthony and was flooded with thoughts. I spent so much time resisting the things that made me unique. I spent so much time doubting them. I strategized around them. I'd do a weird show that went well. I'd have another good idea, but I'd sit on it for a year to space it out. Even my writing packets for professional jobs had backward logic. I submitted a *Saturday Night Live* packet with a bunch of hip-hop sketches. This was while the Lonely Island was on the show and producing tons of great hip-hop-driven digital shorts. I figured I should show *SNL* that I could do what they did.

Why would they look to hire someone who can do what they already have? I never once submitted a packet that showed off the things that *only I could do*. I was doing some of the most unique stuff in New York comedy back then, and every writing packet I ever turned in reflected only bland ideas. I cost myself opportunities, money, and most important, a hell of a lot of time.

Instead of showing off my out-of-the-box impulses, I subconsciously created a habit of snuffing them out. I thought my weird ideas were a roadblock to a fruitful career. In reality, they were my greatest asset. And over and over again, my apologies murdered their potential.

There are things that only you can think of, because you are you and there is only one you on planet Earth. It makes sense that your most unique ideas feel terrifying, because they are creatively risky and also expose the inner workings of your brain. You have to learn to turn off the self-doubt about these ideas. They are the greatest currency you have. Until you learn to erase the self-doubt surrounding them, you will never truly be able to bet on yourself. It is impossible to commit fully to your passions when you can't lower your own defense mechanisms and stop apologizing for them.

Anthony explained another eye-opening aspect of my situation, then gave me a directive that really changed things around for me.

"Do you know that people use your name as the benchmark for weird shit?" he asked me.

"Oh God," I said. "What does that mean?"

"When people pitch me really bizarre stuff, they'll say 'It's kinda like one of those Gethard shows, I guess.'"

I was confused.

"When people want to do cool, strange shit, they use your name as *an adjective for it*," he explained to me. "But you've never gone all in on it. It's time to do it."

I nodded.

"One more thing," he told me. "I'm not letting you hide from it this time. The only way I'm putting this show up is if you call it *The Chris Gethard Show*."

Anthony really changed my life that day. It was yet another example of a true ally seeing things better from the outside and guiding me where I needed to go.

In November of 2009, *The Chris Gethard Show* was born. I vowed to go bigger than I ever had. I promised myself I'd pick the ideas that were closest to my heart—but that I most feared the judgment of—and I'd put them into the world. Before the show premiered I swore to myself: *If I'm going to do this, I'm not going to apologize for it.*

One Saturday a month at midnight a bunch of my strangest friends and I would throw an event that was meant to shock, surprise, and probably fall on its face. The first one featured a buddy of mine, Rob Constance, a beloved member of the New York Brazilian jiu-jitsu community affectionately known far and wide as Black Rob. He's six feet tall and well over two hundred pounds of muscle. I brought him into the UCB Theatre where he demonstrated a series of brutal judo throws and submission holds on me.

We did shows where we intentionally peed our pants onstage. We invited Diddy to appear on the show via Twitter. Inexplicably, he said he was down. He didn't show up for over a year, but it created a strange mystique over the entire idea of the show. We invited anyone in the community surrounding the show to send us names of people they had crushes on. We built a whole spreadsheet and anyone who matched was told live during the show. Two of those couples both dated for many months.

The show picked up steam and I took it as a challenge to go bigger. I thought about the type of person I really wanted to entertain, and what power I thought comedy might actually have. I put a message on Facebook: "I've always been a depressed, lonely person. I'm lucky I'm in New York and have a community. If you're out there feeling those same feelings but you're not in a place where you're surrounded by people, let me know. I'd like to do something cool for you."

A young man nicknamed Fesh got in touch with me. He lived in a small town in Ohio. I flew him to New York and we did a show in his honor. A whole community rallied around one shy overwhelmed kid. *New York* magazine wrote up the evening. I was really proud of it. Fesh now lives in New York. He's started his own comedic wrestling league that performs all over Brooklyn. I'm so happy I was a small step in his story.

At long last real momentum showed up in my creative life. When I stopped thinking about what the powers that be wanted, I made something I thought they'd hate. What it gave me was a growing mass of people who were attracted to something different. I didn't explode into mainstream success, but the framework of a community was there. A lot of people say this era in my life was the birth of a "cult" that wound up following my work. I don't see them as a cult. I see them as a network of dreamers who decided they were bored with run-of-the-mill stuff. I see them as a little minimovement that I am lucky to be the flash point of.

All the good shit started for me when I stopped apologizing for who I was and what I wanted.

Seeds get planted every day. Apologizing for them stomps their ability to blossom.

Many people will get in your way. Don't be one of them.

PUNK

wo and a half years older than me, my brother, Gregg, spent a lot of his childhood annoyed that I was following him around. But I had to. My brother was the guide in my life to everything cool. From comedy to music to everything else worth knowing about, Gregg's always been aware of the hippest stuff before anyone else has ever heard of it. But here's the thing about my brother—he is decidedly not cool. He was born smart, to an eerie degree. He read the newspaper cover to cover before leaving for preschool each morning. A few years later, when most kids were still learning basic multiplication tables, my brother could name the capital of any country on the globe if you pointed at that country on a map. If we were private school stock, he would have had it made. Unfortunately, he went to public school in the dingiest corner of our town. His intelligence put a target on his back and he was ruthlessly tormented by a kid known as Phil "the Bulldog" Monk.

It didn't help that for every intellectual advantage Gregg was born with, an equal physical disadvantage served as a counterpoint. He was born on Christmas Eve, making him by far the youngest and smallest kid in his class. (And leading to a lifetime of him getting shortchanged on presents by me.) He had braces and bifocals by third grade. He was a very brilliant runt who was smarter than everyone else, which wasn't a social asset in a working-class town.

Since life handed him circumstances that meant he was never going to have an inside track to popularity, my brother instead went all in on being an outsider. I thought that was the coolest thing in the world. He ignored all the television, music, and culture his peers liked and instead found out about stuff way beyond his station in life. In the summers he made me stay up late to watch Letterman. When he introduced me to Dave, I was eight, Gregg was ten, but he somehow appreciated the genius of this odd, gap-toothed man wearing suits made out of Alka-Seltzer and submerging himself in a dunk tank. My brother woke me up once in the middle of the night because a cable station was playing a documentary on Andy Kaufman, and we watched with our jaws dropped. I couldn't put my finger on why it was so amazing to watch the fifth lead from *Taxi* insult the city of Memphis, Tennessee, but I knew it was genius because my brother said so. Gregg convinced me to stop watching the WWF and switch over to NWA wrestling, a southern-based promotion where the fighters weren't cartoonish characters but instead tough old scumbags who bled for real and tried to kill each other in every match.

What Gregg gave me most of all, though, was music. He started listening to the legendary (and legendarily odd) free-form radio station WFMU, which was then broadcast from Upsala College in East Orange, a mere two towns away. He was a preteen kid who sat in his attic bedroom next to the radio receiver soaking in Sun Ra, hours-long broadcasts of ambient noise, and commercial-free call-in shows where maniacs ranted about anything that was on their mind. I'd sit and listen with him and quickly learned not to express when I got bored or confused. This would only lead to the dreaded words no younger brother wants to hear: "You don't get it."

If not for my brother, I never would have found punk rock. And like legions of Lower East Side junkies, British working-class toughs, and bored middle-class suburban American kids before me, if I never found punk rock, I imagine nothing good in my life would exist today.

Before you skip to the next chapter, reader who is rolling your eyes, let me be clear that I understand that punk is not for everyone. Some people like songs that are longer than three minutes long, feature more than the same four chords, and don't highlight singers screaming into a mic. I know punk might not be your cup of tea. Some people hear "punk" and still think about English teens with orange spiky hair who wear studded leather jackets and blow snot rockets at the ground while sticking safety pins through their faces. I get it. That stereotype isn't quite true. But I won't waste time trying to convince you, because that's not what matters.

Punk taught me about empowerment. It showed me the strength that comes along with failure. It made me realize that only I can shatter the status quo, the built-in programming that life tries to embed in me. In my opinion, deep down, punk is about two things—asking why things have to be the way they are, and figuring out if there's a way to accomplish things on your own, without the help of any power brokers, or oppressive forces that might dilute your voice and your mission.

You may not be interested in music at all, let alone music produced and consumed by angry teenagers. Maybe you're a midwestern mom who needs to box out more time for your home-based hobbies. This applies to you, too. Because if you ask me, Etsy is the most punk rock website of all time.

I sat in my room on a Friday night, playing *Road Rash* on my Sega Genesis. I developed an obsession with this game, in which you ride in a motorcycle race, brutally hitting other riders with fists and clubs as you pass them. This was my standard Friday night activity that summer between eighth grade and my freshman year of high school. If I'm being honest, it's what I did most Saturday nights as well. Gregg received his license a few months before summer hit, which meant he was gone as often as possible, borrowing our mom's Saturn so he could pick up his friends and take off into the night. My evenings went from watching TV and playing video games with my brother to doing those same activities alone. Worse yet, he'd regale me with tales of his adventures. From tormenting hippies who hung out in a park in Livingston, to nights spent in faraway diners hitting on girls with varsity jackets from other high schools, to scavenger hunts where multiple laws were broken, Gregg had stories of his newfound car-based freedom that made me seethe with envy.

But this night was different. I'd just settled into my postdinner video-game marathon when Gregg sauntered into my room and asked, "What are you up to tonight?"

"Uh . . . nothing," I responded. I wanted to say, *Oh who, me? Just sitting around being bored out of my mind and jealous of you.* I'm glad I bit my tongue.

"Cool," he said. "We'll leave around seven thirty."

"Where are we going?" I asked. He just turned and walked away.

A short while later, we drove up Eagle Rock Avenue. Eagle Rock is the main road in my part of town. My house was a few short blocks from where it ended, meeting up with Main Street. Eagle Rock Avenue, in my mind, represented possibility. It crossed roads that lead to other towns. It led to highways, and those might lead anywhere. Take it far enough and you'd be in Roseland, then East Hanover, and eventually Route 10. From there who knows where? Driving up Eagle Rock meant we weren't staying in our neighborhood. Something was happening.

"Where are we going?" I asked. I was psyched my brother was taking me anywhere. Gregg barely tolerated me a lot of the time. I was annoying. I was his kid brother. I was also kind of a hyperactive angry prick for a lot of our childhood. But he liked that I put him and his good taste on such a pedestal, so every once in a while he'd take me someplace just in an effort to blow my mind.

"Mike D is putting on a concert," he mumbled.

I was intrigued. I was terrified. Mike D was by far the friend of my brother who attracted the most trouble. I'd heard legends about him for years, and before I ever even met him I found just the idea of him very strange and very cool. The first time he visited our house he leaned against the wall near our front door and said nothing. It was as if he feared my parents, or any authority figure really. He wore a leather jacket, had a ponytail, and as far as I was concerned came off as an adolescent mix of Boo Radley and the Fonz. I peppered Mike D with questions.

"Is it true," I asked, "that you once brought a tool kit to school and spent the whole day taking apart desks?"

"Yeah," Mike D said. "Windows, too."

This kid was a rabble-rouser. When my brother said he was "putting on a concert," I didn't know what to expect. I'd never been to a concert in my life. My entire perception of concerts was defined by the video Guns N' Roses put out for their cover of the Beatles' "Live and Let Die." I thought concerts happened in arenas, where sweaty rock stars who somehow pulled off wearing kilts stood on massive stages and blew away tens of thousands of fans. How was my brother's weird quasi-criminal friend going to stage one of those? He wasn't even a musician.

We pulled into the parking lot behind the Pleasantdale Presby-terian Church on Pleasant Valley Way.

"Let's go," my brother said, opening the door.

"Uh, we're Catholic," I said.

"Stop being dumb."

A few kids stood behind the back entrance of the church. At first, I thought they were burnouts, but these weren't the '70s relic stoner types I was used to seeing around town. That gang all had long hair and a greasy vibe and leaned against muscle cars. These kids had on baggy jeans. One of them had bleached hair and a skateboard in his backpack.

We entered the church basement. A small stage stood at one end of the room. Folding tables lined the back wall. Behind them a group of kids was selling stuff. A few dozen young punks were scattered about, including my brother's group of friends and pock-ets of kids who were not from our town. All of them seemed tough. I was the youngest kid in the room by far. It felt a little unsafe.

After a few minutes, there was a commotion onstage. Some kids had climbed onto the stage and were grabbing instruments. I thought they were stealing them. Instead, they plugged them in. One of them stepped up to the microphone.

"Hi, we're the Missing Children," he mumbled. And then, out of their amps blasted the loudest, worst music I'd ever heard in my life. The Missing Children were terrible. They could barely play in time together. The bassist slammed into the singer, knocking him away from the mic, but he still shouted the words, pumping his fist in the air. It was a shit show.

But, man, was it a beautiful disaster. It was perfect.

The crowd rushed forward, slamming into one another, throw-ing their fists up, shouting along with the singer. They didn't even know the words, but so many of the choruses were just things like

"Whoa oh oh" or "La la la, yeah yeah" that you could figure out the lyrics quick and get in on the fun.

It was a sweaty mess. Everyone was caught up in it. I was about to start my freshman year of high school. I was used to doing whatever it took to avoid feeling different. I was a nerd, and as a nerd I stuck with other nerds to avoid standing out or drawing unnecessary attention to myself. That's how I kept life safe, blending in among kids just like me.

That's not how things worked in the church basement, where fat kids spun in circles, bumping up against cool skinny girls. A black skater kid jumped off the stage and landed near a bunch of burly-looking white kids in hoodies. People who didn't know each other had their arms around each other's shoulders. The dancing looked more like a fistfight. But any time someone fell, the crowd would part, someone would help that person up, and they'd hug with grins on their faces. It was like the whole world had short-circuited and everyone was thrilled about it. I'd never seen anything like this.

And best of all, the band onstage was composed of people no different from me. They seemed geeky and resentful and spoke with thick Jersey accents. If we passed them in the hall at school and you told me these kids were in a band, I wouldn't have believed it. The singer wasn't Axl Rose. He didn't have long hair or somehow pull off walking around in a baseball catcher's gear. The guitarist wasn't Slash, a scumbag superhero come to life.

I charged into the group of dancing kids and spazzed out. I'd never danced in public before, but surrounded by kids who looked exactly like the kind of kids I'd argue with in the lunchroom about whether or not Iron Man could beat Wolverine in a fight, I flailed around and had fun. I wasn't hip. I wore an X-Men shirt, not one representing a band. No one judged. No one seemed to even care. Everyone did their own thing, but they still did it all together. It felt great and, I remember thinking, what freedom felt like.

The next band up was called Felix Frump. Their tunes were catchier than Missing Children, and they were less angry, happily dumber. All their lyrics were about how they couldn't land dates. Talk about relatable. Between songs, they bantered into the mic. They were funny idiots, in a good way, and everyone loved them. When Felix Frump played, I danced even harder. My brother stopped flailing his arms around in the middle of the scrum just long enough to make eye contact with me. A grin spread across his face. Here he wasn't the brainy kid with the braces and bifocals. I wasn't the prepubescent runt. We were just two more people dancing, not apologizing, parts of a greater whole.

The final band was One Nature. They were moody. They were intense. They were loud. Unlike Felix Frump, One Nature wasn't messing around. They were still kids—twenty at the oldest—but they were up there because they had something to say, and they were saying it quite loudly. When One Nature played, no one really danced. We all stood in place and listened and watched and swayed and nodded our heads in recognition of our shared anger, which at least for one night, we weren't about to keep bottled inside.

Mike D stood in the back of the room, a smirk on his face. He wasn't playing in any bands tonight. He just put this together so we could have it. He made it happen because he could. For the first time I didn't see him as a troublemaker, I saw him as an organizer. The room was full of kids I'd probably be scared to talk to if I passed them in the hall at school. I realized that's because it's easiest for society to function if people are placed in little boxes. Tonight, these same kids busted out. They all looked different, but what they had in common is that they were all dissatisfied and looking for something. And here, in the dingy basement of a tiny church, they were finding it. Do not doubt the screamed words of musically challenged teens; they might just set you free.

After the show, I was covered in sweat, more excited than I'd ever been before in my life. I didn't want to lose this feeling. I wanted to commemorate this night.

I approached Felix Frump's merch table, which was stacked with T-shirts and cassette tapes. To my surprise, the lead singer was sitting behind the table, selling his band's merchandise himself, something I knew even then that Axl Rose would never do.

I wanted to say something, anything, but the words wouldn't come. I was thirteen. Processing my feelings wasn't a strong point. I had a million things to say, an endless stream of opinions that for the first time ever felt valid. After a lifetime of feeling that the world would be totally fine without hearing anything I thought about anything at all, that night felt like for the first time it might be okay to say them.

"Hey, man, what's up?" the singer asked me.

I looked down, embarrassed. Finally, I blurted out, "I want to be you when I grow up."

He was taken aback. He smiled, then he nodded. Then his face got serious, he leaned across the table, and he looked me straight in the eye.

"No, man," he said. "I want to be *you* when I grow up."

It didn't make any sense, but it made all the sense in the world. I looked back up at the singer. It was as if I saw him for the first time. He and I weren't that different. He was young. He pronounced *coffee* and *dog* "cawfee" and "dawg," just like I and everyone else I knew did. He was familiar, accessible: all of this was. There was no reason I *couldn't* be him. The only difference between him and me was that he picked up a guitar and played it. There was no reason I couldn't learn to play a few chords, if I wanted to. I didn't have to watch from the sidelines. I could participate.

I bought a T-shirt and a tape. I walked away, paused, then turned back.

"Who, uh . . . let you do this?" I asked.

"What do you mean?"

"Like this tape," I said. "It's real."

"Huh?"

"Like . . . you didn't make this by just making copies on a boom-box. It's purple and the song names are printed on the tape and it has a real case and everything. Who let you do that?"

"Nobody, man, we just did it."

My brain exploded. It never occurred to me that you could just *make* a thing. T-shirts? Cassettes? Those come from factories. Adults run those. And when kids want to make dumb shit, adults say no. That's just the way I thought it worked. But maybe not. These idiots had a T-shirt. They made a tape. The other bands both had *records*. Like, on actual *vinyl*. That seemed impossible.

It was the first time in my life that I realized people could just do things, and, if you want them to, things can just exist. No one can stop you if you don't want them to stop you. It *can* be—and is—as simple as that. Now, obviously there are a few compromises that come with this. You'll play in church basements instead of stadiums. You'll have to walk offstage, stand behind a beat-up folding table, and sell your T-shirts yourself. But the things you make will exist.

Learning this changed the way I walked down the street. Everything I saw, I reminded myself—"someone made that." I learned to notice the difference between something that rolled off a soulless assembly line and something that was made with someone's love and passion. I learned young that all rules are negotiable. That night in the church basement is why I had the confidence to do comedy. It's why I felt okay about starting a public access television show when many of my friends told me it would be humiliating to do so. It's why you're holding this book in your hands right now. Life wants us to be embarrassed by things that don't conform to traditional standards. Punk taught me that as long as I'm making shit I believe in, I can hold my head up high. Even if it has to fit in the trunk of my car, it's mine and no one can take that away from me.

So many people are convinced they can't have what they want because someone else told them no, doubted them, or got in their way. But there are others out there, the blue-collar Joes with secret art studios in their basements. Housewives who stopped house-wifing and started selling their wares online. Punk kids who have the balls to shill their music before they even know how to play their instruments. They are the discontented, the beautiful, frus-trated, bored, fed-up troublemakers who say "fuck it" on behalf of all of us. They try, they fail, they try again. When someone tells them how things are, they ask "Why?" When someone tells them something's impossible, they say "By whose standards?" And when someone tells them their idea isn't worth doing, they say "Thank you for your input. Now get off the tracks because the train is coming through."

"I want to be you when I grow up." That's what I told that older kid. "No, I want to be *you*." That was his answer. What a gift. He told me that my dreams weren't as far away as I thought. Though he knew nothing about me, he told me I had potential. I wasn't special. I was just a person. But he let me know there was some-thing inside and he told me I could let it out. Why wouldn't I? Where's the fun in not?

I want you, holding this, reading this right now, to understand: I want to be *you* when I grow up. Chances are you want to unlock something. You have shit to say. You have opinions to unleash. You have products to sell. You've turned to my experience as a guide on how to get you there.

Show me something. Bring your passion to the surface. Don't apologize. Don't wait. Put on a show before you learn how to play. Is failure imminent? Yes. Failure is certain. But don't let that stop you. Failure is a beautiful, inspiring starting point. Punk proves this through and through, time and time again.

I'll be you when you grow up, you be me. Inspire me. Please, for your sake and mine, I'm begging you. Imagine a world where creativity, accomplishment, and satisfaction aren't just the domain of the pretty people, the privileged, the rich, but of regular people making things, expressing themselves, in big ways and small, for one another's enjoyment.

NEVER LET THEM SEE
THE SCALES

Remember that in any field, the basics seem enticing at the beginning. When you don't know jack shit, getting to a point where you know jack shit seems rad, a major accomplishment.

But you don't want to be someone who *just* knows jack shit. Go beyond the beginning.

Back when I was teaching improv, I often found myself flummoxed as to why students would choose the ideas they were basing their scenes on. I realized very early in my teaching career that most bad scenes turned bad within the first thirty seconds. It was rare for a scene that was going great to suddenly go awry. It was usually within the first few exchanges that a scene crapped out. I didn't understand why and wanted to get to the bottom of it. *If so many scenes that go wrong are bad in the beginning*, I asked myself, *how can we build better beginnings?*

I started asking students a simple question: "Why did you choose to start your scene with that idea?"

They'd usually tell me they were using techniques they were taught in previous classes. "Well, these two ideas came up that seemed incongruous, so I thought putting them together would lead to something surprising." "Someone mentioned this thing and I thought placing that idea in Ancient Rome might lead to something." "Someone mentioned moms and daughters so I thought of a situation and started as a mom with a daughter." They weren't technically doing anything wrong. They were executing what they'd been taught. But who cares about showing that you can do what you've been taught?

"How many people," I asked one class, "start scenes with an idea because you personally think the idea is funny?"

Not a single person raised their hand.

My students were very good, but they had developed the bad habit of turning their art form into a math problem to solve. Art can never be math. A plus B might equal C, but that doesn't lead to good comedy. Nor does doing anything by rote lead to anything memorable or worthwhile. The best it can lead to is a pat on the head for remembering a trick someone taught you that you should have thrown away a very long time ago. It's great that you can use the training wheels of a formula to get to something, but who gives a shit if it's not something you believe in? What can you bring to the table no one else has brought before? What's the angle you see that no one else has figured out yet? What's your take on things that's actually surprising and fresh?

Let's say that you want to commit to getting good at basketball. Maybe you played as a kid but were way too short to make the middle-school team, so you moved on and joined the school play, which accidentally sent you down the path to becoming a professional comedian. (As you may have surmised, I tried out for the middle-school basketball team. Anyway, let's keep this hypothetical.)

You kept playing street ball, fucked around with your friends. It was always fun. You went to college and no longer had time to hit the court. You got a pretty intense day gig and never found the time again. But some of your buddies teamed up and joined a league and you wanted in.

The league is way more competitive than you thought. You can barely keep up. Your cardio sucks. You are the guy nobody wants on their team. No one wants to sub out of the game for you. If your team tries to play man-to-man defense, you always get burned, so when you enter the game your team has to switch to zone like you're a bunch of little kids. It's embarrassing.

So you commit. You remember the proper form on your shot. You learn how to dribble with your left hand. You start to shuffle your feet on defense. Maybe you drill in your backyard. Maybe you join one of those weeklong camps for other middle-aged dudes who still dream of basketball glory.

Learn the basics, because the basics help you get good. But the basics don't make you stand out. Let me ask you to consider the thing that makes basketball so fun and addictive in the first place: the creativity.

Your "goals" are to have a better handle, a cleaner shot, a better defensive awareness. But your GOAL is to get to a point where you can get creative with it—to find the unexpected. What's your take on the thing? Can you find one of those sneaky old man post moves that annoy the shit out of the twenty-six-year-olds you play with?

Basketball's a good analogy because of what makes it so unique. I'm obsessed with the NBA. When I watch it, I rarely say, "That person is good at dribbling with his left hand and has solid defensive fundamentals." I say things like, "Holy shit, Westbrook goes into beast mode and no one can stop him," or "John Wall is so fast and his game is *mean*," or most often "Kristaps Porzingis is a golden god. He's seven feet tall, silky smooth, and can somehow still drain threes. He gives me hope that being a Knicks fan might one day no longer be a sad stain on my life."

Creativity blows everyone away. It's the individual stamp a person leaves on a project, event, or any other kind of undertaking. A truly creative individual knows the basics, sure, but it's how he or she puts the basics to use that makes what the person does seem so complicated and beautiful. Whatever it is you set out to do, figure out how to master the basics to the point they become automatic, so you can move on and find something unique that will make people pay attention.

Think about music, too. If you google "How to play trumpet" right now, you'll get hundreds of videos, articles, and links that show you how to purse your lips correctly. How to blow. How to play certain notes. How to put them in order so you can play your scales.

But that will never sell a ticket. Nobody's going to give you their valuable time or hard-earned money to listen to you play your scales.

Do re mi fa so la ti do.

Classical singers sing some version of this tens of thousands of times throughout their careers. Violinists play the scales, saxophonists play the scales, whatever oboe players are called play the scales. Literally every master of every instrument you can imagine endlessly runs through scales.

Play your scales. Make them muscle memory. Turn them from something that needs thought to something that's second nature and instinctive.

Never believe for a second, though, that that's enough. The goal is to turn the basics into something extraordinary, unforgettable, and unique to you and you alone, a true expression of your talent and passion.

Anything someone else can teach you needs to be a plank in the foundation that supports *your own creativity*.

If you can't explain why something is exciting, innovative, new, or mind-blowing, why would anyone else in their right mind think it's any of those things?

Sniff out the unexpected. Fiend for it. The unexpected is where the magic lives. It's how we blow minds.

Don't throw away the basics of your craft. By all means learn from anyone who has something valuable to teach. Soak up information anywhere you can find it. Learn your scales and practice them until you're sick of them, then practice them some more. But when it's time to do your thing, place them out of your mind and do it your way. Acting on the dormant creative fire in your gut requires something more, something beyond the basics, something only you can bring to any endeavor.

Show respect for traditions, worship the old gods, do it with respect. But know that if they have truly empowered you, like all heroes on a journey you must at some point turn your back to them and walk away.

NO NEED FOR ROCK BOTTOM

We all like to imagine that making a change takes on the gravity of a mid-2000s Liam Neeson character's quest. Once we get going, we tell ourselves in our best Liam Neeson whisper, *Nothing's going to stop me*.

But what happens when discouragement sets in?

It's probably reared its ugly head even in the course of your reading of this book. "This is your story, Gethard. Your glory in a middle-school musical has nothing to do with me." Fair. "You don't know my handicaps, my disadvantages." You're right. "This self-help bullshit is for the birds. I'm skipping to only the funny chapters." I get it.

I've never escaped those moments myself. Frustration. Exasperation. Scorn for everyone with a piece of advice. Most times you're likely to get tangled up in these murky moments of trying to accomplish something you might be proud of for once. They're inescapable.

Frustrations will build and mount, and as you'll learn again and again, they won't go away. I can't tell you how to eliminate them. It's impossible. What I can tell you, though, is that I've been there too, many times, and I'll be there again many more.

Rather than eliminate them, you'll have to learn how to coexist with them. The frustrations are your allies. Shaky allies, like Russia in World War Two, but allies nonetheless.

The key to accelerating your growth is accepting that failure, fear, and frustration are not to be conquered.

These frustrations might have you jammed up. They're intimidating. You're buying into them, so much so that you haven't even gotten the gears turning on your dream yet. You've thought long and hard about how to change something in your life. You just haven't found the right time or the right method. Dwelling on your frustrations has caused momentum to feel miles away. The whole reason you're reading this dumb book in the first place is because you're hoping you might read something that precipitates that initial momentum, ignites that first spark. You're hoping I drop a chunk of wisdom that will nudge you over the starting line and into the race.

Fine, I'll give it to you: start right now.

Simple.

"But wait, that's not how this works!" you say. I get it. But my counterpoint would be: It kinda is.

You have to take the initiative to start the process. No one's going to pull the cord on this lawn mower for you. Crank it up until it catches. Starting is on you. We can always let the process of the initial attempt be a simpler and easier one-try right now, see what happens.

You don't want to start because you don't want to fail. Can we not recognize that this is in and of itself committing to failure without even taking a chance?

There are a million reasons not to do something, or set off on an epic journey. Some of them I get. You're already balancing work and school. You have a sick relative who needs a lot of your time and attention right now. Your husband is on shaky footing at work. I'm sure these are true and have varying degrees of actual impact. In these cases, sure, you might be right. I might need to cool my jets. But the point stands in the sense that: you will know when it's time to go for it, and it's on you to pull the trigger. No one else can do that simple act for you.

There is one excuse I'd like to stomp out of existence. It's one that comes up all too often, and it's dangerous for a number of reasons.

I haven't hit rock bottom yet.

You'd be amazed at how many people think that the necessary starting point for something new is when the old life has fallen apart or hit a crisis point to a degree that the only way out is a life relaunch.

I think this is really dangerous.

First, it's troublesome in its effect on you creatively. There's a tendency toward a hero's journey complex when we set out to make cool shit. We view ourselves through a lens; we're this lone wolf taking on the world and going through all the melodramatic steps that come along with that.

The melodrama of what you're doing cannot outweigh the necessity of your hard work. I want to caution against this. Rebuilding a part of your life, or putting something out into the world, is a romantic tale in a certain sense. But the romance of it is nothing compared to the actual act of doing the thing. Only hard work will bring it into existence. Falling in love with the melodrama of your own journey will get in the way of putting your head down and getting it done.

Your desire to change things doesn't need to fit the plot points of a Bruce Springsteen song.

Don't replace hard work with this vision of the grand story.

You can in fact have your life together in some ways while launching into a new phase. Rock bottom isn't necessary.

More important: assuming you have to hit rock bottom before you start invites an unnecessary rock bottom into your life. As a caring and empathetic person, I feel it necessary to step in and say that getting to a point that's scary, hopeless, or unhealthy isn't part of the dream-attacking contract.

My dear friend Mal Blum is an incredibly gifted songwriter. I met Mal after they played *The Chris Gethard Show*. We hit it off and realized we have a lot in common. We both get sad and freaked out and frustrated in the same ways. We've become a piece of each other's support system. Mostly this means going out to lunch together once every nine to twelve weeks. Over kale salads, Mal and I vent our humiliating insecurities without anyone else needing to know about it.

During one such powwow, Mal told me they were thinking of going on antidepressants.

"I really need them," Mal said. "I'll probably be on them like six months from now."

"Wait, if you really need them, why don't you just go and get them?" I asked.

"Well, I don't need them *yet*," Mal said. "Things haven't bottomed out yet. But once they do, I promise, I'll get on them."

"Mal," I said. "Maybe you can avoid the part where you bottom out if you get on them now."

Why give it six months until crisis strikes? Head the crisis off at the pass. Save yourself the misery. Save yourself the rebuild. Get proactive and take care of yourself.

Mal and I have laughed about that conversation a lot. It's so tempting to think that change can't come until it's hit a crisis point where it's *necessary*.

We subconsciously wind up praying for a rock bottom to hit. This is self-sabotage of the highest caliber.

Why fuck up your own life when what you really want to fuck up are the systems making it feel so suppressed?

"IT'S TOO LATE"

In 2004, I got hired as a writers' assistant for a show in Los Angeles. I had to make my way cross-country for it. It was my first real gig. I was thrilled. I was scared. It was the beginning of something.

There was one other New Yorker making the move, a guy I barely knew named Joe. He was hired as a writer for the same show I'd be working for. Because both of us were headed out west, we decided to share an apartment. Our new place was in an odd little complex in Historic Filipinotown. Some people called the neighborhood HiFi. Most people, though, didn't know it existed.

Every morning, I drove us to work, where Joe wrote all day and I took care of all the grunt work that goes into organizing a writers' room: things like ordering lunch and putting index cards on the wall with thumbtacks. People don't know that about television writing rooms—there are so many index cards involved. Index cards are the secret backbone of the entire entertainment industry. If the index card industry went on strike, television as we know it would cease to exist.

At the end of the day, Joe and I always headed home together and talked about how lucky we were. One night Joe even cooked me salmon. He used to give me advice on women, things like "Act hungry and you stay hungry." I provided him feedback on such advice with things like "Dude, I'm not comfortable with this being part of our dynamic."

I was twenty-three. Joe was thirty-eight.

This was Joe's first professional gig in comedy. He left his job as an elementary-school art teacher to do it. He'd spent almost two decades teaching pottery to little kids. On his own time, he did shows, wrote sketches, and learned how to pitch jokes. His first break came when he was almost forty.

He's been a professional writer ever since.

I think of him every time someone throws that very common excuse in my face: "I'm too old. It's too late."

When we're looking to start something, our fear kicks in and we look for reasons to not embark on a journey. I've often had people tell me they feel like they missed their window.

People as young as twenty-one have told me that they feel over the hill. Twenty-six-year-olds hear that and say, "Oh, they have no idea. I wish I still had all that time. But in *my* case . . ." Thirty-five-year-olds hear that and just shake their heads. Somewhere right now, a ninety-four-year-old is shaking her head at a seventy-nine-year-old complaining about being too old.

I don't buy it, at any age. You might have a *lot* of reasons to explain your hesitancy in shaking up your life to go for something. There are responsibilities to family, financial concerns, and so many more very valid reasons to balk. Age isn't one of them. I won't say it's a nonfactor—physical health, energy levels, all those things really do shift with age—but it's the number one knee-jerk excuse we put out there when we don't want to admit the real truth: "I'm scared."

Maybe you want to go back to school but don't want to be the old guy in class. I get it. When I was at Rutgers, a pretty insane ex-Marine took every American history class I was ever in. Every chance he got, he ranted about serving in Vietnam. He once interrupted a lecture on troop outposts in the American frontier of the 1800s.

"The government has a lot of bodies in the ground no one knows about," he told the unsuspecting professor. "I know, I put a few of them there."

He sat front and center, but turned and scanned the room, making as much eye contact as possible.

"What does that have to do with the lesson?" the teacher asked.

"More than you know," he grumbled.

We moved on.

My roommate, Dan, was in that class with me, and we became fascinated by this gentleman. Did we ask questions to bait him into shouting about insurgencies? Of course. Did we once try to follow him after class but lost him when he saw us and began evasive maneuvers? You know it. Did we make jokes about him being the old guy in class? Guilty as charged, I'm sad to say.

But did that guy overcome all of that and get his degree? He certainly did. Age didn't stop him. Somehow PTSD and a general disconnect from society didn't, either, so triple kudos to him.

There are big-time real-world examples too. Jack Roy was a comedian who quit a few years into his career. He started a family and became an aluminum siding salesman. In the early 1960s he said "Fuck it" and, using a new persona, tried again. In 1967, close to two decades after he'd initially quit, he had a breakout appearance on *The Ed Sullivan Show*, which he eventually turned into a huge touring act and, in the 1980s, a pretty great movie career. You know him as Rodney Dangerfield. He was forty-five years old when he made it to *Sullivan*.

John Starks is my favorite basketball player of all time. You may know him as the guy who dunked on Michael Jordan. (Fans of the Chicago Bulls will say he dunked on Horace Grant—fuck that, it was Jordan.) John Starks dropped out of high school to bag groceries. He attended four different colleges. He went undrafted. He wound up on some NBA teams, riding the bench. Trying to get back to the NBA, he played in some minor basketball leagues so small and barebones that they barely even existed. In 1990, Starks was the last man on the roster for the Knicks' practice squad. He was going to be cut. During the last practice of the preseason, he tried to dunk on Patrick Ewing. Patrick Ewing is one of the fifty greatest players of all time. He did not appreciate some scrub like John Starks trying to dunk on him. Ewing fouled him hard. Starks went down and injured his foot. Due to league rules, the Knicks couldn't cut him while he was injured. He wound up playing eight seasons for the Knicks, then bounced around the league before retiring in 2002. NBA players are groomed for success from their freshman year of high school. Sometimes even earlier. A lot of NBA players go pro when they're still teenagers. John Starks didn't stick with a team until he was *twenty-five*. He must have felt fucking ancient. He wound up becoming an All-Star and, over his career, scoring more than ten thousand points. He also got to head-butt Reggie Miller live on national television.

The soul singer Charles Bradley passed away in September of 2017. It was heartbreaking. One of the best shows I ever saw was Charles Bradley's set at South by Southwest. He sang his songs, sweating away what seemed like half his body weight. Half the crowd wound up crying, and Charles Bradley ended his performance by jumping off the stage to hug us each individually. It was beautiful.

Charles Bradley never had an easy life. He ran away from home, bounced around the country doing odd jobs, and supplemented his income by performing as a James Brown impersonator. He dreamed of forming his own band, but the only time he came close his bandmates were drafted into the Vietnam War. This must have felt like a sign from God that he didn't want Charles Bradley to pursue a musical career. Charles never quit, though, and finally a record label noticed him. They released his first record in 2011, which was met with critical acclaim. He wound up having a badass touring career. He was sixty-three when that first record came out.

If Charles Bradley can put out his first successful record in his sixties, you can at least say "fuck it" and give your goal an honest shot before you reach your seventh decade on Earth.

If Rodney Dangerfield can build a career off the phrase "I don't get no respect" in his forties, you can at least try.

And if my friend Joe can ditch his teacher job at thirty-eight years old, write jokes all day, and *still* have time to cook me salmon, you can find the time to make your dream come to life too.

WEIRD N.J.

Spend enough time adrift and feeling alone in your pursuits and you'll eventually cobble together a support system of like-minded people. Mine involves some artists; not just comedians, but also musicians, filmmakers, and other assorted oddballs. I also enjoy the friendship of people with real lives and stable jobs, things like "lawyer," "teacher," "food server," or "public relations guy," but for now let's focus on the dreamers, freaks, and goons who ply their craft adjacent to mine. I lean on them every day. Whenever I fear I've lost my way, I turn to them for counsel. And, while they all don't do what I do, their work inspires me to make mine better. Their commitment to integrity and ideals is a constant reminder for me to never lose sight of my own.

What I'm trying to say is you have to find a tribe. Having a unique idea inherently feels like being alone. Learning how to put your idea into the world can at first feel like shouting into a vast void. But once you break the seal and let out those yells, a funny thing happens— you very often hear the shouts of other frustrated dreamers coming back at you. These people are your allies. They're the ones who get you through times of doubt, who make your ideas better, who inspire you with their own work and their hustle. Tribes of like-minded weirdos interested in the same things as you are always best, and often waiting for you in the unlikeliest places.

The first time I saw an issue of *Weird N.J.* magazine was in the window of Middle Earth, a comic book store on Bloomfield Avenue in Montclair. I wasn't supposed to go to this store. My father came with me once and saw that they had more adult books of the "comix" variety, R. Crumb–type things. Stories with naked ladies and cursing and all that good stuff. I never even glanced at them. I was too obsessed with Marvel to care about anything else. Still, my father was worried that Middle Earth attracted perverts and kindly offered to drive me a little farther to the more above-board Time Warp Comics in Cedar Grove. No one needs to learn about the birds and bees via the twisted thoughts and drawings of disgruntled cartoonists. But I couldn't always wait for him. If he was busy I'd miss that week's releases, and that was unacceptable. There was no chance in hell I was going to wait an extra week to find out if Colossus was going to keep living on Magneto's asteroid in the sky! Comics were my addiction as a kid and I needed them as soon as they came out. I'd sneak to Middle Earth when my dad wasn't around to take me to Time Warp Comics.

One day I walked toward the entrance of the store and froze when I saw the covers of *Weird N.J.* issues eight and nine in the front window. I was transfixed. I'd never seen this magazine before, but I knew in my heart right away that this was for me. I was familiar with fanzines—my early forays into the punk rock scene showed me the joy of reading a homemade magazine someone made for the sake of making it. My pal Mike D put out a fanzine called *Marcia* that brought our little crew some notoriety in North Jersey, and I became very obsessed with a funny zine called *Go Metric* that a band called Egghead made across the Hudson River, in New York

City. To my knowledge, zines were about music. They had record reviews and interviews and poorly written articles in which kids talked shit about bands they didn't dig. This *Weird N.J.* thing I was staring at . . . seemed different. Dangerous. And made just for me.

A bold orange masthead shouted the phrase "WEIRD N.J." Just below it was an image of a grim wall, with peeling paint, in what was a clearly abandoned building. Spray-painted on that wall was a goateed devil head, which stared dismissively off to one side. Next to that terrifying image were the words *Your Travel Guide to New Jersey's Local Legends And Best Kept Secrets*. I could already feel my brain short-circuiting. This did not compute. Someone made a whole magazine about New Jersey? My home state, it seemed to me, was only brought up in mocking tones, never in appreciation. And Weird? What could that mean? I was weird. I'd been called the weird kid in school since fourth grade and I did everything I could to hide my weirdness. You didn't make it part of a title. You didn't shout it to the world from a storefront window. What. Was. This?

The lower half of the cover listed some of the subjects reported on inside. The first listing? "Abandoned Insane Asylums." My older brother and his friends had long told me stories of sneaking into an abandoned asylum on a hilltop a few towns away from us. They called it "The Bin." Stories abounded of lunatics roaming the underground tunnels connecting the different buildings, Satanists who used the building's former chapel for their dark ceremonies, and skinhead gangs that roamed the grounds. Magazines didn't write about stuff like this, did they? Some of the other stories marketed on the cover were described as "Enter the Gates of Hell" and "UFOs, the Image of Satan Cast, and Murder Mysteries *Right in Your Own Backyard*."

I couldn't take my eyes off the magazine. I stood on the sidewalk, staring as the busy foot traffic of Bloomfield Avenue nudged me from behind. If I hadn't walked down that block that day, I may never have found it. But I did. Things changed.

I bought those two issues and read them cover to cover multiple times. The magazine was made by two dudes, both of whom were named Mark. The two Marks made up the entire staff. They were the writers, editors, photographers, the whole shebang. They drove around New Jersey taking pictures of things, the stranger the better: haunted trees, piles of toys left on the side of a road as an unexplained tribute, sewer tunnels rumored to be entrances to the netherworld. I couldn't believe adults spent their time covering stuff like this. And even better, a lot of the articles in the magazine featured contributions from readers. A paragraph would say something as simple as "I live in Springfield. Anyone remember that time a dog went into the woods and came out with a human arm in its mouth?" No explanation, no research, just a bizarre note about a bizarre incident I might never know the actual truth behind. Letters said things like, "Don't go to Midgetville. They throw rocks at your car." What was Midgetville? Though helmed by the two Marks, most of *Weird N.J.* was put together by an entire community. Every article, I quickly realized, was an invitation for readers to participate.

I lived in this place, New Jersey, that everyone made fun of for being toxic and scary and corrupt. And here was this magazine, showing great pride that New Jersey was indeed those things.

From that day forth, my friends and I spent our weekends going on Weird N.J. adventures. We were sixteen- and seventeen-year-old kids, some of us just getting our licenses, and we put them to good use by driving to every haunted corner of New Jersey. On our first such journey, about fifteen of us snuck into the Laurel Grove Cemetery in Totowa to look for a ghost named Annie. The graveyard caretakers shined a spotlight on us and we scattered. My friend Antoine fell down a hill and bounced off a gravestone. He listened to the Cure and painted his fingernails black, and while the experience was horrifying and made him cry, I suspect it was also the greatest moment of his young life. My buddy Steve hopped a fence and in the process cut both of his palms, giving him a sad suburban version of Jesus's stigmata. He was already very tall and skinny, so it really worked for him. Dan Amann never made it back to the car, but I wasn't worried. He was a distant cousin of mine and from Down the Hill, and I knew he was a survivor and a little bit of a maniac. We found him sprinting down the center of Annie's Road, a haunted stretch of street between a river and a canopy of trees, fleeing the graveyard staff. He jumped into my car and we got out of there.

This magazine gave us a chance to basically be West Orange Goonies. We spent weekend nights going on epic journeys twenty minutes from our own homes. It was fun high school nonsense, but I knew even then that it was also an opportunity to look at my surroundings in a different way. Maybe things aren't always what they seem on the surface. And when you realize that about one thing, you understand that potential extends to everything. *Weird N.J.* allowed me to embrace who I was and where I was from. No apologies. It allowed me to look at my world as something to be embraced, explored, and celebrated.

I wrote letters to the two Marks. I told them how there was a high concentration of odd people who walked up and down Main Street in West Orange. One guy dressed as Elvis and pushed a lawn mower all over my neighborhood. Another dude threw pennies on the road and then screamed at them. I sent in my poorly worded descriptions of these people—and one of the Marks wrote back.

"I've seen those kooks!" he said. "I live in West Orange too."

What? This guy was *from* my hometown, and he was making something cool, something underground, something so unlikely? It was this splash of cold water, this reminder that people from the place I was from could actually accomplish things. This magazine

I saw in a random comic book store window was taking on much greater meaning than a homemade magazine should.

The two Marks published my letters about the weirdos on Main Street and another one about a brooding mystery man named Beercan Billy, who lived in the woods behind the bowling alley. I was getting published each issue and becoming one of a regular stable of contributors. "Chris G" was a name fans of *Weird N.J.* came to know, along with other heavy hitters like Ralph Sinisi, a pro BMX rider from Clifton, who offered up many epic tales of trespassing; Pete K., a dude who drove all over the state checking out weird stuff in a converted hearse; and Laura P., who lived near the Jersey Shore and, in the early issues, wrote some of the farthest southern-reaching contributions. This magazine was the source of this very odd community. I didn't know any of these people, but I knew their names and I knew we had something in common. After a life of feeling like a loner who could never quite find his place, I found a thing that connected me with the other loners who never quite found their places either. This was my tribe. I knew I might never meet them in person, but they existed. The tribe didn't hold monthly meetings, but there was a thing, this project, this labor of love that served as a nonphysical rallying point. I marveled at the work of the others who pitched in. They made me want to improve the quality of my own contributions.

And best of all, the community had no demographic. You didn't have to be young and angry to like *Weird N.J.*, like you did with punk rock. Grandmas had letters published. Ten-year-old kids wrote in to talk about how *Weird N.J.* was the first thing that made them like reading. Old, young, different colors, different creeds, everyone was welcome to enjoy and contribute to this thing, as long as you appreciated going off the grid. It was never about how the world defines you, it was about who you really are. It was beautiful. Any time I left the house in my *Weird N.J.* T-shirt, someone unexpected would say, "Whoa. Cool. I'm a real big fan." We were a society of freaks hiding in plain sight.

After a couple of years of having my correspondence published in the magazine, I went out to a slideshow/signing that the two Marks were doing at the Montclair Book Center. Dozens of us jammed into a tiny room to laugh along with them, shout out info about our favorite spots, and celebrate this underground thing we all loved. I was a dorky high school kid, one of the youngest people there. After the event, I waited in line alongside many other grateful oddballs to shake their hands.

I made my way to Mark Moran. "Uh, hi," I mumbled. "I love the magazine. You've actually published a few of my letters."

"Really?" Mark asked. He looked me up and down. "That's cool. What's your name?"

"I'm, uh, Chris G," I said.

His eyes widened. "You're Chris G?"

"Yeah."

"You're a kid."

"Yeah, I know."

"How old are you?"

"I just turned seventeen."

"Jesus," he said. "You've trespassed so many places. . . . Mark!"

The other Mark, Mark Sceurman, turned around.

"This is Chris G," Moran said.

"No fucking way!" Sceurman answered.

We talked about the drifters on Main Street in my hometown for a few minutes, and I left feeling a rare sense of acceptance and even rarer sense of appreciation. It didn't matter that I was this late bloomer little kid. I put in effort, found cool shit, told them about it, and as long as it had value and met the standards they set they published it. There was no ladder to climb. There were no barriers involved. I put in work, I wrote funny stuff, they made use of it. It was a meritocracy in the most real way. A meritocracy that revolved around things like a tower where if you drive around it six times backward, the devil appears in a cloud of smoke before your car, but a meritocracy nonetheless.

At the tail end of my sophomore year of college, I took a chance. This was back when I was working as a "media services" guy at Rutgers. If a projector system broke in a lecture hall somewhere on campus, I went to the room in question and pretended I knew how to fix the problem until this dude named Wayne who really knew how to fix the system could get there. At a state school like Rutgers, some of these lecture halls had four hundred kids in them, which meant I was regularly berated by a frustrated professor in front of a small stadium full of my peers. On top of all that, they made me wear a fucking fanny pack. It wasn't ideal.

Depressed one day while sitting in my windowless media services "office," I shot off an email to Mark Moran in a rare moment of confidence.

"I hope this isn't out of line," I wrote, "but if you ever need help with anything, I'm around and would love to be involved. I have a job right now, but it sucks and I'd love to give my time to the magazine I love instead. No pressure at all. Hope all is well.—Chris."

I'm not exaggerating when I say he wrote back to me ninety seconds later. "Dude—this is nuts. I received your email while I was writing you asking if you wanted a job. Here's my number—call me."

This gig was a dream, but it wasn't easy. I learned one of the great illuminating lessons of my life at that job though: love can make something feel easy, even when it's not.

My primary responsibilities were (1) pick up boxes of *Weird N.J.* issues from a warehouse in Paterson, which was exponentially scarier than any haunted place I visited as part of the job, (2) enter thousands of names into mailing lists, and (3) copyedit hundreds of letters written by teenagers who were almost definitely stoned while writing them.

My least favorite responsibility was our twice-annual mailing list day, when we'd send out mini-issue-style brochures to the dedicated fans. When I started the gig, there were more than five thousand names on the mailing list. I personally licked more than five thousand stamps to plaster on those brochures. By the end of those mailing days, my tongue could have cut glass.

But I also got to write, a lot. If I discovered something that fascinated me, and as long as all the other shittier duties were taken care of, I was free to research and create. I had to break my back at the warehouse—that was nonnegotiable. If I broke my back quickly enough, though, I might have an hour or two at the end of the day to write something that could show up in my favorite magazine.

I also got to drive all over the tristate area dropping off boxes of our issues at bookstores. I would often walk through the store on my way out and see people reading the magazine. Sometimes they'd have big grins on their faces. Sometimes they'd be poring over it intensely, analyzing it like a textbook. Once I saw a young skate punk kid sitting at a table reading a copy across from an elderly woman who was reading her own.

Every once in a while, once the busywork was done, Mark Moran and I would set out on the road and drive around the state to explore all the crazy shit people wrote to us about. Those were the best days. I've been inside a dozen abandoned mental hospitals. I once fell into an underground tunnel while exploring one. I fell down a set of steps in a haunted abandoned home for wayward boys. I also fell down a cliff along a beach in Staten Island next to a crazy person's rock sculptures. Falling down in a lot of cool places was a job requirement.

Exploring is how I eventually ended up cornered in the woods, backed up against a river, as a very large man told me he was going to have sex with me.

The magazine had received a letter about a swamp where a bunch of abandoned cars were arranged in a ring, standing up vertically. That sounds like a pretty great photo opportunity. Call it Carhenge, it's a no-brainer. On a slow day Mark told me to sniff around and see if I could find any info about it. I read the letter, looked at a map, and realized this spot wasn't so foreign to me.

"I'm pretty sure this is a few towns away from where my parents live," I told Mark. "I drove through this neighborhood once—it's definitely strange."

One of the fascinating things about New Jersey is that everyone basically lives on top of everyone, so different cultures aren't so spread out. Suburbs turn into cities, which quickly turn into mountains, which just as quickly turn into beaches, all within an hour's drive of one another. Shady neighborhoods turn into roads that showcase multimillion-dollar homes. A lot of things get hidden in plain sight in New Jersey.

The area we explored was right near the Willowbrook Mall, a commercial hub in Wayne where three major highways intersect. Just a mile or so off one of those highways was an area where two rivers met—and along the banks of those rivers was a very strange patch known as Buttonwoods. People here lived along the river in small houses, keeping to themselves.

"You know the area? You drive then," Mark told me. We got into my beat-up 1986 Chevy Celebrity and drove the half hour from our office. When we crossed over Two Bridges Road, we made a turn and headed down a very narrow street. Even smaller lanes extended into the woods, and the one we went down turned into a dirt road right away. There were tiny houses spread throughout the woods, all abandoned and marked with bright orange spray-painted X's. This area had been messed up in a recent hurricane, and the state was relocating as many people as possible.

But one house was still lived in. No windows boarded up, no government markings, and cars in the driveway—and big glass panes leaning against the house. A car engine on the front lawn, and a thousand other random pieces of junk just piled up everywhere. Not only did someone still live in that house, it was someone who was doing things their way.

Even though this tiny backwoods was only a few acres, those crisscrossing dirt roads could turn anyone around. I took a few random turns. Mark and I were scanning the woods, looking for any signs of the ring of cars, but next thing we knew we were up against the river. And before I could turn the car all the way around, a pickup truck blocked our way back out.

The driver was huge, the biggest man I've ever seen. His hair was white, except for a small patch of black strands, which sprouted out of a very large lump on his head. Slumped down in the passenger seat was a smaller, skinnier guy with a trucker hat pulled down so low we couldn't see his face.

The big guy started screaming at us in a marble-mouthed ramble. "You all come here, little redhead kid in a Chevy, you been stealing stuff, you been—"

"I haven't stolen anything, man," I said. "We just got lost. We're getting out of here."

The giant kept yelling. I glanced over at Mark, who was wide eyed. Mark had seen it all. He'd made his life about going into haunted and dangerous places, and even he didn't know what to do.

The big guy's rants only got more intense. "You come in, you steal, you steal my stuff, all this my stuff, it's like Jerry Springer and all that and—"

I interrupted, a desperation move. "Did you say Jerry Springer?" I don't know why I jumped on that.

"Yeah," the guy said. "I love Jerry Springer."

"Me too!" I said.

He smiled, breaking the tension.

"I love when Steve has to break up the fights," he said, giggling.

"Yeah, Steve!" I said. "Steve's the best!"

"I love when they have the KKK on," he said.

"Sure!" I said. "The KKK!" I hope it's obvious that I do not love the KKK, but one thing I do love is escaping dangerous situations.

The big guy relaxed. He laughed, mumbling about America's all-time favorite sleaze bag television show hosted by a former mayor of Cincinnati. I started to believe Mark and I were going to get out of there, unscathed. That's when the skinny guy leaned over and whispered something in the giant's ear.

"Huh." The driver laughed. He considered whatever idea the skinny guy had put in his head, then smiled and nodded in approval. "Yeah."

"What's going on, man?"

"I'm going to have sex with you now."

He looked right at me while he said it. It was chilling.

"No," I said. "No, you're not."

"I'm going to have sex with you," he told me, "and I'm going to give you twenty dollars."

I still can't figure out why he offered to pay. Did he think making it a transaction would make it aboveboard? Or would somehow imply my consent? Either way, I was insulted at the low offer. Also, I was terrified. No amount of money was going to make me less terrified. I glanced at Mark, who gave me a quiet nod.

I gunned it. My car skidded out into the swamp. The tires spun, mud kicked back toward the river, and I threw the wheel hard to the left. The front end of the car drifted and slid, but I somehow got the front tires back on the road and we finally grabbed some traction. I hit the gas and wound up on the other side of the truck. We didn't get stuck in the mud. Our bodies weren't thrown in the river. Our car wasn't placed standing up with those other cars somewhere deep in the swamp, as I now just assumed those vehicles were this monster's trophies.

We headed out of there, fast. Their truck shifted into gear and made that tight K turn, and I knew we only had a few seconds to get oriented and find our way back to civilization.

Please, I remember thinking. *Let me just make it to the main road.*

The truck caught up quick. It was right on our ass when we hit that first paved road. As soon as my tires caught asphalt, the truck stopped, as if an invisible barrier prevented the truck from emerging out of the woods. We hauled ass out of there.

Business is business, so I wrote up a detailed account of the incident and we published it as soon as possible. The response was huge. People loved a *Deliverance*-style tale, let alone one that took place mere minutes from the Willowbrook Mall. I can imagine a lot of people planned trips involving a nice stop at Borders Books and Music, a swing through the food court to pick up some Sbarros, and then their own foray into the heart of darkness that was Buttonwoods.

We heard from many people who had also encountered the aggressive backwoods truckers. A cop wrote us and told us he once had to arrest the big guy, who was so strong that he flexed and broke the handcuffs. A lady told us she used to live back there and loved it but had to move because these same two men terrorized her and kidnapped her dog. Another kid got chased, but he wasn't as fortunate as us. They chased him all the way down the main road. To shake them, the kid was forced to drive the wrong way down a highway against oncoming traffic.

After a few years, the letters slowed down. Then out of the blue, one more came in. This one was from another cop.

"The guy you called the Beast of Buttonwoods died this week," he told us. "I figured you'd want to know. Not just for closure, either. I knew those guys. Dealt with them a lot. They were brothers. Troubled, but good guys underneath it all. But more importantly, Schulzie always got a kick out of reading about himself in your magazine. He was a really big fan of *Weird N.J.*"

The thing I'd always loved most about *Weird N.J.* was that it birthed a community that paid no attention to age, gender, class, race, or any other demographic slot. It was for everyone. Even, apparently, the monsters we wrote about.

Weird N.J. showed me an invisible network of writers, photographers, artists, troublemakers, and oddballs. Your tribe is out there too. The frustrated, scared, fed-up people who desperately want to say something. Find them. They're out there. For me, it took a random day where I stood on a sidewalk and stared into a window at a magazine cover and my jaw dropped. Maybe your tribe is in your own backyard too.

If you're in a small town where it seems like no one's interested in hearing what you have to say, you can't be the only one who feels this way. Find another weirdo. Cling to them. Support them, even if their goals are different from yours. You may have nothing in common beyond frustration, but frustration with the way things are is a great starting point for creating something big. Build a network of like-minded allies. If you're in a massive city feeling like you're drowning because the pace is relentless and no one has an ounce of humanity in their soul, find the other oddballs who are in the same boat and keep each other afloat. There are concerts and galleries and exhibitions and performances happening every night—these are just some of the other places where you will locate the other discontented dreamers who have something to say. They're sitting in front of laptops in coffee shops right now with a grimace of frustration on their face. Find them. Support them. Let their existence support you.

And when all else fails, there is the internet. On the average day, it's a cesspool of fighting and cynicism and snark. But at its best, it brings us all together. No matter how bizarre, how unique, how particular your interests are—someone out there shares them. Unite.

Get out of the house and participate. Get out of your own head and be a part of a bigger movement. Get out of your own way and find a community. As an individual you *might* be able to make an impact. But, as a member of a community, that power and potential increases exponentially.

A community is out there for you. Connect with it. There are allies to be found, wars to be fought, trenches to hole up in together. You can incubate one another's dreams and then watch them die together. Cheer for one another's failures and see what's on the other side.

It's easier to survive beautiful disasters when you have allies in the cause. Friends and compatriots remind you that when your world burns you should stand right next to the flame. Fires are warm and, sometimes, they light the way.

"NO ONE WILL GET IT"

One of the frequent and convenient dream killers we often lean on is the good old "No one will get it anyway." We have an urge to make a thing, but we're scared that we might fail. Because of this, we convince ourselves that failure is inevitable, that its arrival is imminent and, most likely, embarrassing. It gives us an excuse to not try.

First of all, this puts the cart before the horse. One of the fundamental rules of creating something: *it's not up to us to decide how the world reacts to the things we make.* In the early days of creating, we think the process goes something like: "First I'll make it, then I'll get it out there, then they'll react to it in *x, y,* and *z* fashion, then that momentum will lead to the next thing, etc."

In truth, we only get to lay claim to those first two steps. Make the thing. Get it out there. That's all you can control, and that's all you should want to control. In art and in everything else, people get to decide what we create means to them. Stop worrying about what people think and make your shit.

Making stuff and not caring about the reaction is easier said than done. But here are some notable examples from which we can all learn about creating something new out of nothing, simply for the sake of making it.

Henry Darger was a janitor in Chicago. He was also a hermit. He lived like a recluse in a small apartment on the North Side. He made some people in his neighborhood nervous. They didn't know that he would one day be embraced as one of the greatest artists America has produced.

Henry was hospitalized at a very old age; he died in 1973. His landlords, in an effort to find any documents related to sorting out his belongings, or contacts for next of kin, entered his apartment. What they found was remarkable: several hundred scroll-size watercolor paintings, depicting kids and warriors and exotic landscapes. A lot of the drawings are of girls with penises.

His paintings are beautiful, trippy stuff. I've seen some of them in person. I've never been cultured enough to really appreciate visual art. Museums feel stuffy to this lowbrow Jersey-raised grandson of Irish immigrants. But these blew me away.

The paintings, it turns out, are illustrated portions of another work of Henry's: *In the Realms of the Unreal*, a 15,145-page novel he wrote. He worked on it for six decades beginning in 1909. You wonder how he had so much time. I do too. That's what makes it all the more stunning that he *also* wrote a separate ten-thousand-page novel called *Crazy House*. All ten thousand pages were hand-written. Oh wait, he also wrote another book called *The History of My Life*. It began with about two hundred autobiographical pages followed by close to five thousand pages about a tornado.

Now, Henry Darger was, to put it mildly, an odd guy. His work doesn't make much sense in any traditional fashion. Who knows why he made it then hid it. Maybe it was the manic output of a damaged mind. Or maybe he thought no one would understand.

Here's the thing: today, he's hailed as a genius. He's the poster child of outsider art. Museums have embraced him. Scholars have studied him. He never even meant for his message to be sent, but when it was, it was received in dramatic and positive fashion. He had an impact on the world, when he only meant his work to be seen by himself in one room in Chicago.

In 1968, three sisters from New Hampshire formed a band at the behest of their crackpot father. Their names were Dot, Betty, and Helen Wiggins, and they called their band the Shaggs.

Austin Wiggins, their father, convinced a prophecy foretold that his daughters would form a popular rock band, removed his daughters from school, bought them instruments, and made them record an album.

That album, *Philosophy of the World*, gained no traction upon its release. If you listen to it, you'll soon understand why: the Wiggins sisters hadn't learned much in the few months they prepared. The songs are atonal. The rhythms don't make sense. The lyrics are chanty and strange. Put simply: the Shaggs are hard to listen to.

But a few years later, Frank Zappa—a renowned musical genius—was a guest on the Dr. Demento radio show. He announced he was going to play some songs he loved, and he put on the Shaggs. No one knew what to make of these songs, but the album became a collector's item.

Years later, it was reissued and became the focus of fierce debate. Reviews sometimes mocked it. But others hailed it. Many laughed it off. Others said it was genius. And some of those who embraced it were pretty big deals—Kurt Cobain once listed it as his fifth-favorite album of all time.

Is the love for the Shaggs sometimes ironic? Sure. But others swear by it in genuine fashion. It's art that made people talk, made people think, made them reconsider how they consume music. It's strange, it's weird, it's funny, it's great, and it's awful. But it's not what anyone expected, and it's sold a lot of copies. Austin Wiggins's prophecy proved true.

"But, Chris," you might say to me, "to create without fear of consequence, do I have to be an insane hermit or the victim of an abusive dad?"

"Not necessarily!" I reply. "You could also be a blind Viking who worships Norse gods!"

If you walked past the corner of Fifty-Fourth Street and Sixth Avenue between the 1940s and early 1970s, chances are you encountered a very tall blind man dressed in Viking warrior regalia banging drums, playing a flute, or manipulating homemade instruments.

This was Louis Hardin, better known by what I think might just be the greatest nickname of all time—Moondog. This blind Viking is a man we can all learn from, and we should aspire to be like him.

We've all seen street musicians. Some of them are fantastic. But some of them seem like unhinged people. A blind Viking playing arrhythmic tunes set to the backdrop soundscape of New York City street traffic certainly would seem to fit the bill for the latter.

But Moondog wasn't homeless. He had an apartment *and* a country estate. And he wasn't talentless. In fact, he's been hailed as a genius. Was he a bit nuts? I don't know, I never met the guy. But I do know that he dressed like a seafaring marauder from the Middle Ages and worshipped Thor. I'm sure that being blinded in an industrial accident didn't do anything to make his mental stability *better*. But, tellingly, Moondog's supporters and friends weren't crazy. They all recognized talent when they saw it.

In the 1950s, disc jockey Alan Freed stole the name Moondog and started using it while playing the Viking's recordings on the radio. He was trying to take his persona as his own. Moondog sued him. Some of the people who testified on Moondog's behalf, vouching for his talent and the quality of his work? Benny Goodman, jazz legend. Arturo Toscanini, a vaunted classical musician.

One of his earliest champions was the conductor of the New York Philharmonic. Philip Glass said that he learned more from Moondog's work than he learned during his time at Juilliard. Moondog had chops. You or I might hear his street music and think it was bonkers. But people who knew music on an intrinsic level were blown away. Those who understand their craft to a degree I never will bowed at his altar.

In the 1970s, Moondog moved to Germany, where he was embraced. He made hundreds of compositions and toured the world.

If anyone ever made stuff for the sake of making stuff, it was Moondog. Has anyone ever given less of a shit about how stuff was going to be perceived? Not only was his music dense and hard to understand, he gave himself the added handicaps of playing for decades on a street corner and *dressing as a fucking Viking.*

Has anyone ever taken their insane amount of talent, multiplied it by their (in his case literal) handicaps, mixed it together with his remarkable quirks, and made shit more purely? I don't think so. Moondog had true skills. He also had a true vision for what his music should be. That vision didn't match at all with what any sane record label, agent, or middleman would ever want to invest in. He didn't care. He literally took to the streets. He let everyone think he was crazy. He made his art, didn't apologize for it, and made sure his music was heard on a busy street corner in one of the most crowded cities in the world.

When you're making things, you have to Moondog that shit. You don't need to dress as a Norse warrior or pray to ancient gods. But you do need to find a way. When every venue slams its door in your face, you have to be ready to take it to the streets. When no one wants to help you, you have to help yourself and bring what you have to offer directly to the people. And most of all, you must scrub yourself clean of the need to justify the existence of your art.

Make it. If no one wants it, force it. That's what Moondog did. And for decades no industry respected him—but his peers did. Real recognizes real. Art doesn't need to be successful to be embraced. Dream your dream, enact it, then get out of its way. Your dreams don't owe anything to anyone, not even you.

DUSTY BUNTER: TRUE SCUM

approached adulthood with all my influences mixing together: strong examples of people embracing chaos and working hard, taking pride in being different, and secure in the knowledge that communities of outsiders can band together. You'd think I'd be poised to let those ingredients stew together, merge and bubble to the surface, until I became the fully formed DIY comedian who's cobbled together the somewhat respectable career that you now see in front of you.

You'd think that, but you'd be wrong. Instead, I betrayed all those ideals.

One of the core things I'd learned was to trust my own instincts. Punk isn't about doing things the right way, it's about doing them your way. *Weird N.J.* reiterated the value in doing it myself. I'd learned to place integrity above all else and to run through a wall to make things happen. There are no shortcuts!

But then a shortcut offered itself up and I jumped at it. I learned a new fundamental rule: you are going to need help in life, so make sure that those who offer to help you aren't only helping themselves.

In any field, you need support. No matter how much of a trail-blazer you are, there are mentors, allies, men and women who inspire you to take your chances. In my world of entertainment, you pretty much need aid in the form of managers and agents. You can't find gigs without them. One of the early distressing turns my career took involved a professional dalliance with one of the strangest people I've ever met. This is a cautionary tale. A tale of woe. A tale of suffering. This is the story of the most through and through scum fuck I've met in my close to two decades of doing comedy.

I started comedy in New York City when I was twenty years old. I looked like I was sixteen. There are people in my world who spend their days plotting ways to make cash off others, and that was my moneymaker: I looked young. Looking that young was an asset, because it allowed casting agents to circumvent child labor laws. Why pay an actual underaged kid to play an underaged kid, what with all those fees and nosy parents, when you can pay a twenty-year-old who's still going through puberty? I wasn't always funny in my early days, but I retained the appearance of a kid who just got stood up for prom. There was potential there.

One Friday morning in 2002, I was at work, driving a van around New Jersey and dropping off boxes of magazines. It was hot. I was tired. My phone rang.

"Hello?"

"Chris, it's Dusty Bunter."

Every now and then someone starts a conversation with an unearned sense of familiarity. This was one of those situations. Sometimes it takes me a second to place a name, but there was no way I would forget a prior conversation with someone whose name was as ridiculous as Dusty Bunter.

"Okay," I replied. There was an extended silence. He expected me to say more, but I had no idea who this person was or how he got my phone number.

"I'm a manager," he continued. "I saw you at the Upright Citizens Brigade last night and I think we can do some real damage together."

This was interesting. I was doing comedy because it was the most fun thing in the world to me. People around me were starting to taste success. That success was enticing. When I saw other performers show up in commercials, I wondered how to get in on it. When I realized people were paying their rent via comedy, I was jealous. Paying the bills via the dream? Sign me up. I needed help breaking into that world, and here out of nowhere was this mystery man offering me his assistance.

"Wow," I stammered. "That's uh . . . that's great. I'm sorry, I'm driving. I also don't know how any of this works."

"Here's how it works!" he said with what I now look back on as unnecessary force in his voice. "You're fresh faced. Young. An All-American boy. And I think we can make a lot of money off that."

Reading it back now, that is one supercreepy thing to say. But back then it was exciting. Someone saw the talent inside me and wanted to help me unleash it unto the world. Dusty was dangling that all-important word out there: money. The auditions started right away. He asked if I had a pen. I pulled over to the side of the road and scrawled an address down on a piece of filthy cardboard I found on the floor of our van.

"Tomorrow, ten in the morning," he told me. "Sign in under . . . Magic Hat Talent."

The first audition Dusty sent me on was a Sprite commercial that would only air in South Africa. It was a bit odd, the "only in South Africa" thing. Seemed shady. But I didn't think too hard about it. Who was I to question someone who was trying to help me out?

I took the day off from *Weird N.J.* to audition for the commercial. Later in the day, a breathless Dusty gave me a call.

"They loved you!" he told me. "They fuckin' loved you!"

I was on "first refusal" for the commercial, which means the production company requests that an actor or actress hold the dates because the production is really close to hiring you for the gig. Casting was down to me and one or two other actors. Dusty told me to have my passport ready—a trip to South Africa might be in my near future.

That didn't come to pass. They went with some other dork with freckles. But Dusty flipped out. His instincts had been correct: I had cash-earning potential, baby! He was high on me and pounded the pavement on my behalf. I was getting at least one audition a week. I was overwhelmed but thrilled. Who would have thought that I, a confidence-lacking kid from Jersey, could get this close to the big city dream?

I did notice, though, that I never signed in the same way twice. For my first commercial audition, I signed in under "Magic Hat Talent." For the next, I signed in under "High Peak Entertainment." Sometimes I signed in under "Top Flight Management."

I finally asked Dusty why I was always signing in under different company names.

"That's just how it goes," he told me. "We gotta keep 'em on their toes!"

I didn't know what that meant. Keep who on their toes, exactly? And to what end? I reminded myself that I was just a rookie. I had to learn to trust the veteran who was Dusty Bunter.

Getting a lot of auditions was great, but I had a full-time job. In New Jersey. So every time I had an audition in New York, I had to take off a whole day of work. My boss wasn't thrilled. I knew I was pushing it. But I had a dream, and I was chasing it.

One day I was driving my work van when I got a call from Dusty.

"Got a good one for you tomorrow," he told me.

"I don't know, man," I said. "I've been taking off work a lot and none of these are panning out. My boss is pissed I leave so much."

"I get that, I get that, I do," Dusty said. "But this one tomorrow—you gotta do it. It's perfect for you. They're looking for someone who can play young. That's you! This was meant to be."

"Fine," I said. "I'll work it out."

"Great," Dusty said. "Sign in under Impresario Enterprises."

The next day I skipped out on work. I sat in Lincoln Tunnel traffic fighting my way into Manhattan. I paid more for parking than I usually spent on a week's worth of food. I made my way to a casting agency. The place was bustling—lots of kids were running around while their parents yelled at them or gossiped with each other. The confusion made it hard to find the sign-in sheet.

"Can you point me toward my audition?" I asked the girl at the front desk.

"We're only running one session today," she said. "Right over there."

She pointed at the pack of kids and stressed parents. I made my way back toward them.

I guess this phase of their day must be wrapping up, I told myself as I wrote my name down. *I must be the first one for the next group they're seeing.*

About fifteen minutes later, my name was called by an exhausted casting assistant who barely looked in my direction. I walked into the audition room. A camera was set up and three agency hotshots sat behind a table. I walked in. One of them saw me and did a double take. Confusion washed over the faces of the other two.

"Can we help you?" one girl asked.

"I'm here to audition," I said.

They looked at one another. Then at me.

"Who sent you here?" the other girl asked.

"My manager," I said. "He said you were looking for someone who could play young and thought I—"

"The part is for a seven-year-old boy."

"Great, thanks, sorry, thanks, bye, I'm so sorry."

I grabbed my coat and bag and ran. I could feel the eyes of distrusting stage moms locked onto the back of my head. I mashed the elevator's call button. That thing could not come fast enough.

Minutes later I was on the phone with Dusty.

"You didn't even read that shit!" I yelled. "All those moms thought I was a fuckin' molester or something! I'm twenty-one, man, you just made me audition for the part of a seven-year-old!"

"Look, dream big, no apologies, my man," Dusty said. "I'll have something else for you soon. Something great."

That day came a few short weeks later. Dusty told me there was a Doritos commercial I'd be great for. I begged off another day of work. Another schlep into the city. Another crammed hallway full of aspiring actors.

Only this time, I couldn't figure out what the type was.

I'm not offended when I show up at some casting agency and there are a ton of nerds there. That's how commercials go. Sometimes they want you for your talent, but a lot of times they want you because you look vaguely like Anthony Michael Hall and someone paying a lot of money for the ad is a *Breakfast Club* fan. I've sat shoulder to shoulder with so many other dudes who wear glasses. So many guys with ginger complexions. Dozens of people with improv backgrounds. I know my type. You meet your type. After a few years of auditioning for commercials you pick up on who's in your circuit. There is an actor in New York named Jeremy Redleaf. He has red hair and glasses. He's really nice. I know he does performance art stuff. I know he makes films. I know a lot about his career pursuits and life. I have only met Jeremy at commercial auditions. We have only spoken while killing time waiting to audition for some shitty role. I have gleaned a lot of info about his life and creative pursuits, twenty minutes at a time, while we wait to audition for Geico ads. Outside of a casting house, Jeremy and I have never spoken (except for one time when we randomly ran into each other at the Mohegan Sun casino).

This Doritos audition, though . . . there was no rhyme or reason. An obese black male actor sat next to a little pixie Zooey Deschanel–ish white girl. People of all shapes, sizes, and backgrounds were here. Short, tall, male, female, young, old, every type of person was waiting to go in.

This must be one progressive-ass casting agent, I thought to myself. *These people have nothing in common.*

Except for the gloves. A disproportionate number of these actors were wearing gloves. Indoors. It wasn't winter or anything.

And they all seemed to know one another. It's one thing to be in a room that's unexpectedly diverse. It's another to realize that in the same way I knew all the glasses-wearing gingers, this gang all seemed to be very aware of one another.

A redheaded girl emerged from the room where auditions were taking place.

"How was it?" a Hispanic dude asked her.

"Simple," she said, "no body or face or anything. Just the hand and the bag."

"Excuse me," I whispered to the actor sitting next to me. "Is everyone here auditioning for the Doritos commercial?"

"Uh, yeah, kinda," he said. "It's not a commercial. Modeling. It's an ad. A print ad. For the newspaper."

"Oh," I said. "I've never done any modeling."

"I don't do much either," he said. "Hand modeling just clicked with me though. Turns out I have nice-ass hands. Got lucky, I guess."

The alarm bells went off. The gloves. "Just the hand and the bag." That's what these people all had in common—they had beautiful hands.

Dusty Bunter sent me on a hand modeling audition.

Now, that may seem bad just on the basis that I am a comedian and not a hand model. It gets exponentially worse. I have a genetic condition called nail patella syndrome that affects certain joints—my elbows, knees, and HANDS. Specifically, I have no top knuckles. They exist, but there are no lines on them and I can't move them. My fingers are straight little nubs that have a claw-like quality. Sometimes people watch me on television and tweet comments at me, something like, "Yo, your hands freak me out." I respond with, "Why did you tag me in this?"

It's not just the knuckles. Why is my condition called "nail patella syndrome"? First off, because it messes with your knees, hence patella. But "nail" refers to fingernails. I was born with deformed nails on my thumbs and both index fingers. The index fingers feature triangular slivers of nail with huge splits down the middle. Both my thumbs have a nub of nail, about one-third the size of a normal person's, and the rest of the nail bed is cratered in.

I'm fine with this state of being. It is what it is, and rarely does anyone even notice. Unless, of course, they're taking a professional-quality close-up picture of my hands for potential placement in various publications.

I can't imagine anyone is very interested in having my lil' claw hands be the public image of Doritos.

I stormed out.

"Dusty, what was that bullshit?" I yelled into my phone from the sidewalk out front.

"What?" he asked. "Did you crush it?"

"It was fucking hand modeling, dude," I said.

"Okay. So?"

"I was born with mutant hands," I told him.

"What? Like the X-Men? Huh?"

"Not like the fuckin' X-Men!" I snapped. "Dude, I took a day off work. You can't send me somewhere and not tell me it's hand modeling. I don't know about you, man."

"Look, I get excited," he said. "You're right, I should have read the casting notice more carefully. But I'm just excited *about you*, you know? I think with a little attention on you, the world is yours."

I took a deep breath. *He's just trying to help*, I reminded myself. *Be grateful and move on.*

I promised myself I'd keep my guard up in case Dusty ever got in my way again. It was starting to dawn on me: *this individual might not have my best interests in mind*. I was ready to sniff out more sleazy behavior. Turns out, I didn't need to look very far.

The last audition Dusty sent me on was pretty relaxed. The casting house wasn't packed with desperate people. Things were quiet and running on time. I got to my audition ahead of schedule, which meant I could grab the script and run the lines a few times before I went in. I was alone in the waiting room and able to take a deep breath.

Until another actor came in. I had my eyes on the dialogue and was trying to focus, but this guy was distracting. He dropped a pen while signing in. When he bent over to grab it, the contents of his bag spilled on the floor. He cleaned up, then let out a wet hacking cough. I tried to ignore it but had to see for myself who this train wreck was. I glanced up over the edge of my script.

It was Dusty Bunter.

"Dusty?" I asked.

"Chris, hey yeah, what's up, man?"

"Not much. What are you doing here?"

"What do you mean?" he asked.

"Well . . . you sent me here to audition, right?"

"Yeah."

"I've never heard of a manager coming to the actual room," I

said. "Are you supposed to drop in, make sure everything's running smooth or something?"

"Oh, no bro," he said. "I'm auditioning too."

"Excuse me?"

He made deep eye contact.

"Everybody's gotta eat, bro," he said. "Everybody's hungry.
Nothing personal. May the best man win."

I auditioned, then waited days to hear from my manager if I
was beaten out for the part—by my manager.

I stopped answering Dusty's calls. My middleman was holding
me down. He was blocking my way. The shady son of a bitch was
literally competing with me!

Remember: There are a million Dusty Bunters in this world. People ready to grab on to you for their own gain. People ready to say
the right things to make you think they have your best interests
in mind when they're just trying to make a buck off your hard
work. The leeches are out there and you never need to look far to
find one.

I committed from that day that I'd accept the help of others,
but only if they could really help me. And there are good inter-
mediaries out there. There are people who love you and admire
what you do and want to help you get better. They will champion you. They'll earn your trust. They will make every effort to
advance your career because they become legitimate teammates,
and because they believe your efforts deserve more spotlight and
success. There are people who will get in your corner and be the
fiercest defenders you ever have. When you find the ones you can
trust, grab on to them and don't let go. Always remember that
when it comes to facilitators for your career, it's not about what
they can get you—it's about the goals and ideals you both share.

And walk away from the cancerous souls who only want to ride you to wherever you're going. I've seen so many people fall into the trap of feeling like they *need* the support of people who don't have their best interests in mind. I've had so many friends wind up in shitty situations with agents holding them down, but they won't leave. Why? Because they don't have anyone better. "I'll wait to fire my agent until another agent seems interested." No. Cut out the cancer and move on. No one better is magically going to come to your rescue if you don't seek them out.

The only one who will help you is you. Help yourself now, so better people can help you later.

I have no idea if Dusty Bunter booked the part we were both up for that day, because I didn't speak to him for seven years.

Then one fateful afternoon, I was exiting an audition. As I gathered my jacket and bag another actor entered. He signed in. I stared from across the room. He tensed up. He felt my gaze locked on to him. He finally turned and looked deep into my eyes.

"Wait," he said. "Do I . . ."

It had been almost a decade. He couldn't place my face. I'm sure there have been dozens—if not hundreds—of young naive actors since me who he's sunk his claws into before they realized he was malignant, human quicksand.

"Don't I know you?"

I stepped toward him and grinned, never breaking eye contact.

"No, Dusty," I said. "You don't know me. We've never met before. Let's just both go on our separate ways and pretend none of this ever happened, okay?"

I pushed past him, bumping shoulders. He looked confused to his core. As I shuffled past the sign-in sheet I leaned in and read it. Right there was his name, in bold block letters. DUSTY BUNTER.

He signed in under High Peak Talent Management.

BITTERNESS IS THE ENEMY

There's nothing less attractive than bitterness.

Failure can be a mark of pride. It can be the cool scar that you have a war story about forever. You *can* meet defeat with your head held high. This is possible.

There's nothing less appealing to me than going to a bar with a bunch of comedians who talk shit about more successful comedians. The smack talk really flies when a more successful comedian is also younger than those talking the smack.

The older bitter types love to say that those in their crosshairs have the hype, the looks, the youth, but they don't have the chops. "It's easier for her to get that writing job because everyone's looking for diversity these days!" It couldn't *possibly* be because that person turned in a better packet than you, could it? Ninety percent of the time, the shit talkers don't work as hard as the shit talked.

Take all the time you'd be tempted to sit around and spit venom and use it toward the betterment of your craft instead. One builds you up. The other tears someone else down. Building yourself and your skills up might actually get you somewhere. Tearing someone else down doesn't change your own momentum one bit.

It's hard to accept on the most desperate days, but another person's success has nothing to do with your failure. It's too easy to point fingers, to blame outward. If that person you have in your crosshairs didn't get that job, it doesn't mean you would have. If you're the type of person who spews up bitter bile, you probably weren't a close second anyway. Your priorities are mixed up and you've let ego and anger become massive roadblocks.

Venting frustration is healthy and necessary. Directing anger at undeserving targets isn't the same thing. One is an honest way to let negativity go so you can move on. The other is a way to make an excuse for your own failure. When you make excuses for your failures, you lose the potential to let failures teach you something.

I have seen many examples of marginally talented people who work hard, improve themselves, and endure many early failures who eventually break through and make something of themselves. I have seen exponentially more examples of *very* talented people who make up excuses, begrudge others their success, and spread word of how unfair it is. I have never witnessed one of these people turn it around and go on to great things.

Failure can be your greatest ally, your most profound teacher. It can show you things about yourself, your process, and your goals that you had no idea of. Failure can lead to beautiful introspection.

It can also turn you into a bitter turd. Simply put: don't let it.

GREGGULATION

Gut checks are a very important step to install into your routine. In pursuing your own avenue of attack, you will at times feel lost and overwhelmed. You'll feel helpless. You'll be unsure of what direction to turn. Nothing seems productive.

This is when you need to touch base with real life. Seek out things that inspire you.

If all you think about is the thing you want to accomplish, it can quickly turn into an obsession. It rolls in like cloud cover and dominates your view of everything. To succeed, you need to put in a daunting amount of work. A natural by-product of this is that the work comes to dominate your time, life, and attention span.

If all you think about is your own art, what the hell will your art be *about*?

I highly recommend finding inspiration and productive distractions in people working in different fields than you are, but who are also in similar stations. Seeing someone execute their own dream can be a rallying cry that gets you feeling positive momentum again.

There have been times when I felt totally jammed up and useless. That's when I like to walk away from my own art. Oftentimes, this means seeing the efforts of other artists creating in my sphere of influence. I'll check to see if my friend Jeff Rosenstock is playing any punk shows near me. Any time my friend Antonio Campos has a film out, I see it and expect to walk away energized and inspired. If I want to keep things closer to home and find comedic inspiration, I'll go watch my friend Mike Birbiglia. He tells stories onstage, too, but he transforms them from stand-up sets into well-thought-out and directed shows, and picking apart the craftsmanship takes my mind off my own writer's block for a while.

When your world feels like it's closing in, remember that the world is infinitely bigger than you. These are the exact moments to take in the work of people you admire. By immersing yourself in their work you can stave off existential crises.

One of my most profound experiences with this involved watching my own brother, Gregg. Just as he was as a kid, Gregg is very much an outsider. He still knows about everything cool. And he still likes to cause trouble from the outside looking in. At one of my most stressed-out points, where I'd really gotten my priorities mixed up, a performance of his helped put me back on the right path.

It reminded me what it's really like to not give a fuck. What it means to make something for the sake of making it. What it means to embrace failure. Gregg's performance has become akin to a weird rosary bead for me, something I pray to for guidance when I start to feel lost. When I feel my priorities shifting in the wrong direction, I take a deep breath and rerun this evening in my head.

I was in the middle of a long stretch where my work was jammed up. I couldn't get new jokes out. I'd start writing projects and they'd peter out. I was strategizing a lot, figuring out which projects might lead to results that would make them worth my time. I was blocked.

Gregg called me one day, worked up. When my brother speaks

with a manic intensity, I know he has something good planned.

"There's a club down here in Philly," he told me. "They barely book local comics, and they never book the artsy ones."

"Okay," I said. "But that happens everywhere. Why do you sound so exasperated?"

"Because they run this dumb fucking competition," he told me. "The winner gets to perform at the club throughout the next year. And I hate it. All these comics who are friends, who support each other for eleven months of the year, get all shitty and competitive with each other. I hate what it stands for."

"Well, there's not much you can do," I said.

"I think there *is* something I can do," Gregg told me. "I'm going to ruin it."

"Don't tell me another thing," I said. "I want to be there to see this for myself."

The night of the show, I made the trek to Philly. The club was packed, standing room only. Drinks were flying. The club must have been making money hand over fist. I crammed into a booth with my brother's small group of pals.

The competition featured a wide range of talent. This wasn't a meticulously curated contest; if you could get some asses in the seats, you could compete. Some of the comics were taking the stage for only their second or third time. They were nervous. This was a big, raucous crowd. Some of these young comics stepped up admirably; others crumbled, forgetting their jokes and giving in to that sweaty panic. As a fellow comic, I empathized. There's no feeling lonelier than bombing. There's no sensation worse than standing in front of a microphone and realizing you don't remember the second half of your own joke. For a lot of these comics, that would be the last time they ever set foot on a stage.

But it wasn't all newbies. Some seasoned vets came in and delivered smooth, practiced sets. They had solid jokes, great delivery, unquestionable timing. Some of these comics were young and hungry and impressive. This competition meant something to them, which I had to admit was cool to see.

After a dozen or so performances, my brother's name was introduced over the public address system. He walked out to center stage and took a deep breath. He scanned the crowd and located our table. A slight smirk, almost imperceptible, spread across his face. He took one last look across the rest of the room. I know my brother well enough to know what was going through his head: *Should I really do this?*

He approached the microphone with supreme confidence and shouted, "YOU ARE ALL WITNESSES!" It was loud. Jarring. The crowd shut up.

This was during the same stretch that LeBron James would start each of his basketball games by walking to the scorer's table and throwing a giant pile of powder in the air. It was iconic at the time. My brother took a bottle of baby powder out of his pocket, poured a massive mound into his hand, and threw an explosive cloud of white dust over his head.

This club was perfectly built for stand-up. Like all great comedy clubs, the ceiling was very low. The powder bounced off the ceiling, which was no more than eighteen inches above my brother's head, coating him and causing him to have a hacking coughing fit—not the best way for a performance to start.

Best of all, the dust storm billowed out into the club. Audience members recoiled as it hit their clothes, their hair, their eyes. It landed in people's drinks. One guy stood up and shouted, as loud as he could, "FUCK YOU, DUDE!"

The powder even went into the vents of the air-conditioning system that crisscrossed the ceiling of the club. As the dust circulated, it began falling softly, covering pockets of the club in a light snowfall.

People weren't just mad; they were *furious*. My brother's strange conceptual performance was always going to be a tough sell as part of a competition in front of a drunk crowd at a traditional comedy club. But he'd gone beyond anything I'd imagined and dug a very deep ditch for himself before the first punch line.

I was laughing so hard I couldn't even focus on my brother's attempts to tell actual jokes. He shouted, a lot, while the audience continued to seethe. Gregg tried to keep their attention as people wiped baby powder off their clothes in a rage. The room was a swirl of grumbling, angry movement, and daintily falling powder. People cursed from the back of the room. My brother shouted over the din.

After a few treacherous minutes, he took a deep breath. He was approaching the end of his time, and now he needed to stick the landing.

"You've been a good audience," he declared. "And as such, I shall grace you with gifts!"

Then he reached into a bag and pulled out a T-shirt with his own face printed on it. It was not well made. It seemed like a shirt that had been worn before and not washed. The picture of his own grinning head was ironed on at a strange angle.

My brother signaled, waving his hand in the air. "Minions, come to me!"

Two guys stood up from the table I was sitting at and sprinted to the stage. My brother reached back into his bag. There were tangled cords sticking out. He was having trouble removing whatever was wrapped up in there.

It popped out—one of those metal lamp shades you see clipped up at construction sites. My brother asked one of his "minions" to hold the cone as he removed two bungee cords with hooks on the end.

He fiddled with the hooks, placing them through holes in the sides of the cone that he'd clearly punched in himself. Before doing so, he hadn't consulted the rules of physics. The holes were different sizes and not lined up across from one another. They were just gnarled gaps in the metal with sharp, jagged edges. Each of his goons took one of the bungee cords and stood on opposite sides of the stage, stretching them to their limit.

He'd built a gigantic slingshot.

He placed one of his bootleg T-shirts inside his even more bootleg-launching device. As he pulled it back, the front row erupted with shouting.

"Don't point that fucking thing at me!"

"What the fuck? What's wrong with you?"

These people had serious—and very founded—concerns. Gregg's slingshot was going to come apart and fly into the crowd. The closest audience members were seated less than three feet from the stage. From the back of the room, I could feel the movie moments playing out in their heads: that disc flying through the crowd, rotating wildly and beheading them. The bungee cords coming loose, whipping out into the crowd and fish hooking their cheeks, snapping back and pulling their mangled faces back toward the stage.

Gregg had now infected the audience with multiple emotions they weren't expecting from a comedy show: confusion, anger, and fear. The only thing he hadn't given them was laughter. T-shirts flew at high velocity into people's faces. To avoid the projectiles, people ducked under tables. When they popped back up in a rage, their drinks spilled, their half-eaten baskets of mozzarella sticks tumbled to the floor.

After launching a half-dozen T-shirts, my brother's time was up. He grabbed the mic.

"Thank you so much! Vote for me!" He said it with a cocky grin. He scooped up his equipment and walked off the stage. Most people grumbled. Some outright booed. A handful of us cheered.

The silence afterward was shocking. This was a contest. A new comic came out every handful of minutes, assembly line style. There were no pauses. There were no breaks. There were certainly no stretches where no one was onstage and no music was playing. The murmur slowed down and it was silent; no drinks clinking, no talking, just a totally quiet club sitting in the aftermath of comedic destruction.

Then, yelling.

It came from backstage: faint at first, the muffled staccato sounds of rage. Then, high pitched, my brother's voice trying to answer before being shouted back down. You couldn't make out words, but you could hear the passion of the conversation through the Sheetrock.

Then some audible words slipped through: "Go! Now!"

My brother reemerged. He looked into the crowd, who were as angry as ever, and took a deep breath. He was carrying a roll of paper towels and a spray bottle.

He sauntered back to the stage, his head hung low. He sank to his hands and knees and scrubbed the performance area free of powder.

Then, for the first time since he took the stage, there was a laugh. Then some more. Then a wave of mocking, jeering chuckles.

The crowd hadn't laughed with my brother, but they were now very willing to laugh *at* him. He'd been forced to come out and clean up his own mess. It was pathetic. They loved it. Mixed in with the laughter were victorious, vicious jeers.

"That's what you get!"

"Fuck you, loser!"

"Buy me a new drink, dick!"

Gregg finished wiping down the stage, stood, and gave a quick wave to the crowd, most of whom renewed their boos, though a few audience members applauded.

He did not win the contest.

My brother can be a destructive force. But as a creative soul, he is pure. Is it cool to destroy something like a comedy contest because you don't agree with the morals behind it? Probably not. One could simply not participate, or vent in private, or do any number of things that would lead to fewer dry-cleaning bills and a growing blind fury in which other comics would have to perform.

But to my brother's credit, he realized entering a contest because it might lead to something was anathema to the idea that creativity and community should always supersede success.

As my brother crouched on that stage, cleaning up a physical mess he created while enduring the audible dissatisfaction of a crowd he'd infuriated, a realization came to me. I occasionally made good things. But I didn't care enough about those things for their own sake. I cared too much about what they might lead to. I cared too much about what the people around me were getting. I had to stop giving a shit about such concerns. I had to embrace the work. Every ounce of energy focused on anything outside of the work was wasted, fat to be burned.

Seeing Gregg's show was like taking a hot shower. The next time I got onstage I was looser. I was willing to play around more. I tried new material with more reckless abandon. I experimented.

Seeing the work of others can motivate your own. When their work is good, it wakes you up. When their ideals mirror your own, their work kicks you in the ass and makes you move. And when you watch people you admire taking chances beyond what you've ever dared imagine taking yourself, your own goals don't seem so bold, let alone frightening.

PUBLIC ACCESS

've told you to do it for yourself, yet I'm also asking you to put faith in me. I've told you to be wary of anyone who says they can get you closer to a dream, yet I'm trying to show you that very path. I've implored you to ask, over and over again, if you can trust the people you meet along the way. So I hope you've been asking yourself this whole time: *Can I even trust* this *asshole? He's talking the talk, but has he in fact walked the walk?*

I have indeed.

I mentioned earlier that I was cast as the lead in a sitcom, which was called *Big Lake,* in 2010. If anyone looks at my present-day life and asks, "How did he get there?," they're not referring to that sitcom. No one watched it. No one envies that experience.

That all went down ten years into my career.

So before we even discuss what it's like to endure an epic public flop, understand that ten years of hard, unrewarded effort went into just getting the chance to endure an epic public flop. Before you even get a chance to fail, put in at least a decade. Don't stress about why it's not happening until you've put in years; if you haven't, that's probably why it's not happening.

Also consider that after the flop, it took four full years of rebuilding in the aftermath before things really got cooking in my career. But when they did, they got good. For the past four years, I've actually been feeling pretty good and secure. Podcast. Television show. Stand-up career. Three strong pillars that have given me more strength than I thought possible in my world. None of those were close to happening for four full years after my public failure.

Never forget that as you read anything else here. It took ten years to even earn a chance to fail big. It took almost half as long to bounce back. Nothing replaces time. Nothing replaces work. And most of all, nothing replaces resilience.

With all that in mind, let's take a closer look at what it's like to bomb.

As a refresher: It's 2010. Jon Heder, a movie star who played the titular role in the beloved cult classic *Napoleon Dynamite*, decides he doesn't want to be the lead of a sitcom he's been cast in. This show has already been picked up for ten episodes. Production is up and running. Writers, producers, a lot of people have already been paid. No one wants to lose their money. They decide to cast a replacement.

I—a total unknown who lived in a bedroom with no closet and slept in a disassembled IKEA loft that once made my dear friend Don Fanelli sit me down in concern and say "Dude, get your life together, you sleep in a fucking dog bed"—am cast in the lead role last minute. For the second time in my life, I am the last-second replacement for a much cooler, safer bet of an actor. In eighth grade it was the Fonzie of my middle school, Danny Tobia. At the age of twenty-nine it was the dude who popularized VOTE FOR PEDRO T-shirts.

The show bombed.

I could spend pages explaining what happened throughout the

production process. How it was disorganized. How everyone was flying by the seat of their pants. How communication between the production team and the writers and the network never really lined up. How things moved at a pace that was impossible to keep up with and the whole thing was probably a hopeless case from the start. I could throw people under the bus, beat myself up along the way, all that jazz. I wrote those pages out. It was cathartic. But it was gossipy and ultimately, I think, useless. The thing to focus on is what life is like on the mountaintop. The tl;dr version? It's as good as you hope it is in that sleazy Hollywood way.

Getting the part wasn't just a long-awaited career break, or an ego-affirming validation, though it was very much those things. It was also a financial transformation. Cash, baby. Cash.

"It's a weird type of deal," my agent told me. "Ten episodes guaranteed. If they pick it up beyond these ten, contractually they have to do another ninety."

"That's crazy," I said into the phone.

"The day it gets picked up," he explained, "you'll make two point two million dollars."

Two million dollars.

It was dangling in front of me. If I got that money at the age of twenty-nine, I could probably make it last for most of my life.

I fought for ten years to get a chance. I got the chance. I'd spent ten years wondering why my friends all got gigs and I didn't. Ten years feeling bad about myself, and here was my shot! Money was on the way. And the validation came soon after. The *New York Times* wrote a profile on me, wondering who I was. Newspapers, blogs, the story of this underdog coming up from the underground was everywhere. People were finally paying attention.

It was intense. Man, was it addictive.

There were girls. I will be graceful about this part, as I know both my mother and wife will read this. But I was single back then and there were a lot of articles being written about me. I'd never been confident with women. When you look like a grown-up version of the kid from *Jerry Maguire* and are also riddled with anxiety, you're probably never going to be mistaken for a ladies' man. That all changes when you start getting press for being the next big thing.

I couldn't go on Facebook after midnight without someone hitting on me. It was insane. The first time it happened, a message popped up from an acquaintance. She was a pretty Brazilian girl. Out of my league in a big way. She made money modeling. This was not someone on my radar. I'd always thought she was beautiful, but never even thought about asking her out.

"I saw your girlfriend at the Brooklyn Lyceum the other night," she typed.

"I think you mean my ex-girlfriend," I replied. "I've been single for months."

"Oh good," she replied. "That's what I was checking on. When are you taking me out?"

Things like that kept happening. Jen was a pixieish blond girl who always dressed superfashionable and had a moody mystery about her.

One night I got a text from her at about one in the morning.

"Hi."

"Hey," I answered. "Everything okay?"

"Yeah . . ."

"What are the dots for?"

"Nothing, I guess . . ."

Then there was a long pause. I wrote again.

"If there's anything you want to say, you can say it. I won't be mad."

"Do you want to come over right now?"

I went to her house. She came from old money. She lived by

herself in a huge loft in Manhattan that had been in her family for generations. Oil paintings of her ancestors lined the walls, and best of all, her bed was positioned beneath an oil portrait *of herself.* She also had a grand king-size bed. This is a bed that is even larger than a king-size bed. I'm not kidding, there are beds bigger than the beds you know about. They only tell rich people about them.

We fooled around a bit, then she abruptly stopped.

"I want to show you something," she told me.

She left. I sat awkwardly in her bed, mostly undressed, staring at an oil portrait of her. I picked up the book on her nightstand. It was titled *A Glossary of Financial Terms.* She came back around the corner, her naked body standing in the doorway, backlit so I could only see her silhouette. She was holding something. I squinted, unable to make it out. It squealed. I jumped.

"This is a hedgehog," she told me.

"Why do you have a hedgehog?"

"I stole it," she told me. "From a man in Korea. I had to hold the hedgehog under a sweatshirt, all the way back on a flight from Seoul to New York."

"You smuggled a hedgehog?" I asked her.

"Yes," she said. "I smuggled a hedgehog."

The most intense relationship of this stretch was with Rebecca. She and I shared a brief but very passionate stretch of time together. She sent me a Facebook message at 2:53 a.m. on April 10, 2010. It read:

"Hi! I saw you tonight at McManus! I am a huge fan, but I was so distracted by the crazy guy who owns the place that I didn't get a chance to come over and say how excited I am for you. I can't wait to see the show. And maybe one day I'll actually have the opportunity to say this to your face? Maybe buy you a Dr. Pepper? Whatever."

I wrote back, "Thank you! Yes please to the Dr. Pepper."

I didn't hear from her for months. Then one night she signed on again.

"I don't know if you remember me," she said. "But I once offered to buy you a Dr. Pepper. I never came through on that. Anyway, want to come over?"

We dated for three months.

Money. Girls. I was really living it.

None of it changed the fact that the show wasn't going to be good.

We filmed two episodes each week. Scripts weren't completed until the day of filming. I'd be given a full script the night before. I would be explicitly told, "Don't bother reading this, the whole thing is being rewritten."

I'd wake up to find scripts in front of my door. Some poor PA had to drive out to Woodside in the middle of the night to drop that day's off, ostensibly so I could start memorizing it before I left in the morning. I learned not to memorize *these* scripts either. It was a waste of time.

There would be a script waiting for me in my dressing room when I got there. *That* was the script we'd work off of (and more rewrites would happen throughout the day). I'd walk in, someone would ask me what I wanted for breakfast, and I'd set about memorizing a forty-page script that we were going to shoot about seventy minutes later.

Luckily, I was taking a drug called Nuvigil. This drug should not exist. There's no way it's healthy. It turns people into more than people. It was created to combat jet lag. In reality what it does is turn you superhuman. I'm not exaggerating when I say that I could read a script three times through and have it memorized. I was able to memorize forty pages in about thirty-five minutes. I could also do this on three hours' sleep, which was often my state of being—the by-product of my newfound dalliance with the aforementioned Rebecca. I once read a rumor that there were sections of Afghanistan that US soldiers were unable to take. They'd give them Nuvigil and they'd overrun the places in no time at all. This drug was bonkers. It didn't make me all that buzzed, either. The only side effect was it made me pee more often than usual. When I wanted to go to bed, I'd just lie down, decide to go to sleep, then be out. I later learned that they based the entire plot of the Bradley Cooper movie *Limitless* around this drug.

Add weird drugs to the money and girls list. I was living the life.

None of that changed the fact that the show was a flop. The reviews were brutal. Many of them blamed me. No one cared that the production was flying by the seat of its pants, or that the writing process was the definition of chaotic. I was the public face of the show. I took it on the chin. Professional reviewers creamed my performance. As you can imagine, internet comments were even worse. One guy posted on my IMDb message board that my agent should kill herself. People knocked not just my performance, but my personal appearance. I was mocked, scorned, beaten down—and all I had done was work for ten years, then taken my best shot.

A few days after the cancellation I woke up, expecting to be depressed. Instead, I felt awake and energetic—and I hadn't even taken Nuvigil. It hadn't been two weeks since the show was deep-sixed. It wasn't like me to bounce back. I walked into my bathroom, looked in the mirror and said out loud, "You don't even like sitcoms. Why did you fight so hard to be on one?"

The words poured out of me. I hadn't ever crystallized that thought before. But it's true—there wasn't one sitcom on television that I enjoyed watching. It made me think back to 2007, when I was a guest writer at *Saturday Night Live* and, after they didn't hire me for the next season, I had a nervous breakdown that sent me back into therapy and onto antidepressants for the first time in years. I grew up on *SNL* and respect it greatly, but I hadn't watched it regularly for years. Why did I let it mess with my head so bad that I didn't get offered a job at a show I wasn't passionate about?

And why did it fuck with me when my friends got gigs and I didn't? I just wanted a thing that they had. I wanted validation. I wanted to be recognized as good enough, as equal to them. It didn't matter that the jobs they were getting—and sincerely, more power to them—weren't things I had any personal love for. I just wanted things that other people had for the sake of having them.

It was ego.

It was envy.

It was petty.

It was not the attitude that should be found in someone who spent his adolescence at punk shows, and his twenties working for an underground fanzine. It wasn't me.

When the depression and humiliation passed, when the pipeline of bad reviews slowed down and no longer stung, I wound up on the other side feeling alone and exposed. But I also felt unburdened for the first time in years.

I was free. Life had marched me right up to the edge of a dream, and the whole thing tumbled down just in time for me to realize the dream I was trying to achieve wasn't what I wanted or needed.

When I took a breath and realized I'd maybe dodged a bullet, the world all of a sudden felt full of opportunities again. Opportunities for things that were smaller, closer to my heart, things unique to me. I felt like the kid entering a church basement again, remembering that the world was full of opportunities I could haphazardly run toward.

Now it was up to me. Would I get back in the ring? Would I fade away? Either one felt viable. Maybe I didn't have to get back in the ring; maybe I could still attack this comedy thing while forgoing the ring and going off the grid entirely. Maybe I could remember why I got into this game. It wasn't for money. It wasn't for girls. It wasn't to take pills that eliminate your need to sleep or eat. It wasn't to get patted on the back. I got into it because I felt like my head would explode if I didn't get to make shit I cared about. Maybe this was a lesson in what happens when you lose your integrity. I was at my professional rock bottom. My first shot was as big a miss as I could imagine. Waiting in the comedy club green room with other comedians, I could feel their pity. Ten years of work and it felt like it was all down the drain. I had to start over. When I looked past the shame and embarrassment, though, I knew: that restart was a blessing.

Because maybe this time around I could remember who I really was. My failure showed me how far away I'd drifted from my own priorities. I would never let that happen again. I had no idea if I'd ever get another shot that big. I swore to myself, though, that this time I would trust my gut and do it my way. If I was ever going to get creamed in the press again, it was for damn sure going to be for something I believed in. I'd been put on my ass. Somehow, though, the knockout blow woke me up.

When I signed up for a public access show, some of my friends expressed concern. It was a dead medium. I was blowing my momentum. It seemed so desperate.

But still, I managed to round up some collaborators. They tended to be younger people with chips on their shoulders that rivaled my own. My friend J.D. Amato agreed to direct the show. Another old friend of mine, a guy I'd worked with a lot over the years, told J.D., "You don't want to do that. It's not going anywhere. Don't attach yourself to Gethard's midlife crisis."

I'd signed up for the show in the first place because this guy Keith I played basketball with pulled me aside one day.

"I work at the New York public access station," he said. "I think all the weird shit you do onstage would be a really good public access show."

I was sort of insulted, but very intrigued. I grew up loving local TV. I always thought public access was underground and cool and strange. Keith told me I could do a live show and take phone calls. I was obsessed with call-in shows as a kid. My brother and I spent no small amount of time pranking them. When Keith told me that everything the studio did was streamed live online, an alarm sounded in the back of my brain. *That's actually pretty modern. Anyone can find that. There's a shitload of potential there.* And when he told me the studio was free to use? Sign me up.

I took to the environment at the Manhattan Neighborhood Network like a fish to water. People made shows that were *of them*. There was a mother-and-son team of producers who made a show about chamber music. They used the studio before us some weeks and always made me and my crew marshmallow treats. They were supercool people, as nice as you'd expect a mother/son combo who loved chamber music to be. Pockets of people from different New York neighborhoods made shows that represented their economic realities, their ethnic backgrounds, their relationships with local government. It was real-life grassroots activism in real time. This place gave voice to the voiceless. It allowed television that would never be given a chance in the traditional industry the ability to live. There were also *tons* of yoga teachers.

Don't get me wrong—there were also a lot of maniacs involved. I loved that even more. The day I entered the studio I was told a story about an alleged high-ranking gang member who had a show for years but was now banned from the studio because he threatened to kill a staff member. Keep in mind, he was still allowed to have a show. He just wasn't allowed to use the MNN studio. He had to pretape his work. Each week he'd stand at the corner and call the studio, over the legally required hundred yards away. A member of the security staff would meet him and collect a VHS tape of his show from him. The station broadcasted it. That's how much these people support free speech and limitless creativity: they let you have a show *even if you threaten to kill them.* There was a show that followed ours that was just close-ups of naked ladies dancing. And not just boobs, either. Full butthole. On one show a lady interviewed an admitted child molester about how he was visited by angels and can travel between dimensions. Turns out that anything goes on public access. That had great appeal to me following my experience doing a sitcom on Comedy Central.

The audience that had been selling out *The Chris Gethard Show* each month at the UCB Theatre didn't come with us. I was washed up and people weren't interested in watching me flounder on an outdated medium. We struggled through our first episode, a live hour-long broadcast full of miscues and failed bits, all while confused audience members shifted uncomfortably in the seats. We all wore black and white thinking that was a cool stylistic choice. Instead it looked like a religious cult was putting on an unfunny comedy show on the surface of the moon.

But toward the end of the hour we got a phone call from a guy named Walter.

"I don't know what this is," he said. "I was flipping through the channels and whatever this is, it's confusing. But you guys are kinda funny, I guess?"

We made a thing and sent it out into the world. Someone received the message. Some guy named Walter. It starts with one. He was our only fan. But we had one. It had begun.

For over four years, a growing gang of cronies and I showed up every Wednesday night at the Manhattan Neighborhood Network studio on Fifty-Ninth Street between Tenth and Eleventh Avenues in Manhattan. We made stuff there. We created some of the worst dreck I've ever farted out. But we also created some work that I'm fairly certain I will never top.

Our episodes were more miss than hit, but we pulled off a few things in the early days that I was proud of, that showed off my philosophy of what I thought television could be. One episode involved me being brutally beaten down by a professional kickboxer. It looked crazy on the surface, but I was sending the message—"I don't want to have a talk show where the host is in control. I'm at the mercy of all the other forces at play here." Life had beaten me up the year prior; I was turning that into something literal, something creative, something inventive.

We let the audience call in and boss us around. We played games that fell apart and had the most fun when it did. We invited comedy friends to come hang out, and some of them actually took us up on it. Horatio Sanz, my ally, my defender—he stopped by and lent his name to our ramshackle show. He'd hang out and take calls with us. We started seeing tweets about the show saying things like, "Why the fuck is the dude from SNL a part of this shitty thing?" It wasn't exactly praise, but people were finding it. Cipha Sounds is a legendary DJ from Hot 97, New York's culture-defining hip-hop station. He was starting out in comedy and we crossed paths. I invited him on the show, and all of a sudden people realized a tastemaker was opting into our odd little cult. Hip-hop fans were so confused that he was there. But they were checking out the show.

I remember the first time I saw someone post praise about our show online. There was a comedy message board known as "A Special Thing" that I used to check from time to time. Lo and behold, one day I saw a topic titled "The Chris Gethard Show." A young lady named Caroline E. Anderson posted that, "This show isn't perfect . . . but there's something here." I sent her a note of thanks, and on the next episode wrote on a T-shirt with a black marker:

"Caroline E. Anderson is the shit." Caroline is one of the first of many people who reached out in the early days of our show and said they connected to it who went on to chase their dreams. I mailed her that shirt. She said when she was a kid in Texas, our show made her think that maybe making things was possible. She moved to Los Angeles and is now a professional comedy writer. I'm happy that our bizarre run on public access television is so often cited as a point of inspiration for young and hungry comedy kids who didn't think they had a chance at taking it to a professional level.

We started getting more ticket requests—I saw this firsthand, because I was the person single-handedly answering all those emails. During our first few months we'd get at best a couple dozen people asking if they could come hang out in the studio. Sometimes we'd have episodes with less than ten people in the audience. It steadily grew. People were shocked that I answered the emails myself. Someone would ask, "I was hoping for four tickets," and I'd write back, "Yeah, sure, here's the address. Say hi when you get there so I know who you are.—Geth." I once got an email back from a guy named Keith Haskel that said, "That's rad that you wrote back yourself. That's real deal shit." He introduced himself to me at that week's show. He was wearing a banana costume. He came all the time. I later learned that he was a highly sought after postproducer and editor in the world of NYC television comedy. I asked him to work on our show. He had shown up one day as a fan who liked weird shit. He is now a coexecutive producer of *The Chris Gethard Show* on truTV.

I started getting emails from a kid named Patrick, a student at Pace University, who showed up each week with half a dozen girls. We were confused; who was this doofus, and why did he roll with a harem? He was young, but kept telling us he wanted to work on the show. He dragged his friends all the way out to the west side to check this dumb thing out and we really appreciated it, so we let him help lug stuff around and erect the set. We had him show up, move chairs, all the grunt work stuff. We almost fired him because any time we managed to get a famous person to swing by our studio and appear on the show, he bothered them for pictures. He was like a fiend for selfies, and we couldn't trust him around celebrities. He's now the celebrity guest booker for *The Chris Gethard Show* on truTV.

One day, I noticed a burly guy with a beard moving wires. I had no idea who he was. Each week I'd see him lugging sound equipment, setting things up, helping out. I asked J.D. if he knew who this guy was. "Nope," he said. "I think his name is Dave." We didn't know if he worked at MNN or what. He never introduced himself, he just appeared one day and started working harder than everyone else. One Wednesday he showed up wearing a shirt advertising Rutt's Hut, a hot dog stand I used to go to in Clifton, New Jersey. I asked him about it. "I'm from Jersey too," he said.

"Cool," I answered, "then I guess your name is Jersey Dave."

It turns out that Dave's gig was traveling around the country filming dance pageants. He'd constantly get on planes so he could travel to strange venues in small cities to chronicle on video stressed-out children dancing in an effort to please their overzealous and sometimes aggressive stage moms. Needless to say, this job stressed him out. He wanted to move on. He had insomnia one evening, found *The Chris Gethard Show* on public access while flipping through the channels, and that night he sent me a drunken email claiming he could "make your show bosser." The next week he showed up to volunteer. Jersey Dave is now one of two segment producers on *The Chris Gethard Show* on truTV.

"The World's Greatest Dancer" Rob Malone. Andrew "Hot Dog" Parrish. Random Orlando. They're all people who wandered into a public access studio one day and I now am fiercely proud that they have a job through my efforts to bully my show onto "real" television. These were people who were all to some degree or other outsiders. Keith was a pro who wanted to work on the weirdest stuff possible. Patrick was a kid who didn't know how to find his way in. Dave's job was driving him insane. My idiotic show became the life raft for all these weirdos, who just happened to show up, looking for their tribe.

Longtime callers and online fans moved to New York to work on our show, which still blows my mind. Fred from Honolulu is now a researcher on our show, and one of the most fascinating, smartest people I know. Royce from San Francisco is a PA. He used to call our show to explain Bay Area slang, like the word *hyphy*, back when he was a teenager. Now he works here. (I still don't understand what *hyphy* means.) We knew Sarah Davis only by her Tumblr name: Laughterkey. She used to post a lot of stuff about our show and helped make us very popular on Tumblr when the platform was at the height of its relevance. She was just a fan, a faceless internet handle on a screen. We later found out she lived in Florida, where her day job involved doing back-end programming for an "international dating" website. I'll let you read between the lines on that one. She now lives in New York City and is our show's social media manager.

The knowledge that I built a thing that made weirdo kids feel safe taking chances will always be a point of pride.

Things grew. We took it to a scrappy young network named Fusion. We'd survived. Now we're on an actual national platform: truTV. We clawed our way up the food chain. And kids from all over the country who probably wouldn't work in TV without it have their first gigs. Sink or swim, this aspect of the show is the thing I am most proud of. Our best episodes and greatest comedic moments pale in comparison to the idea that these people found a thing. Back in the day I learned how to find my tribe through the music I liked and the magazines I read. My failure facilitated the fact that this time, I created a tribe, out of nothing.

The public access studio was these kids' church basement. This show was their *Weird N.J.* I was lucky enough that the lessons I'd learned while young were still dormant somewhere inside me. Chasing ego and money and girls had gotten me nowhere. That behavior was a betrayal of who I was at my core. I ran in the opposite direction and built something that other people took the same lessons from that I learned as a kid from the outsider artists who inspired me. The people who became a part of my work came to occupy someplace between friend and family. We stayed united. That unity has been my safety net ever since.

I stopped worrying about the ego. Instead, we made it about the work. But even more so, we made it about the people.

We made T-shirts. My house was overrun with them. The people at the Greenpoint post office—both consumers and workers—grew to hate me. Once a week, I'd show up with dozens of packages. The return address was my real home address. I put a handwritten letter of thanks inside each package. If you ordered a T-shirt from me between 2011 and 2014, you had my home address, knew what my handwriting looked like, and could steal my DNA off a licked envelope. Oftentimes when people ordered something they'd put in a note along the lines of, "I can't quite pinpoint why, but this show is really helping me." I'd put a note in their envelope saying, "That really means a lot, but I promise you it's helping me even more."

This was far from the days of women picking me up online. It was a trunk full of crap and dragging sacks of envelopes to the post office. I was losing money instead of making it. It was heaven.

We got invited by small theaters around the country to take the show on the road. Usually they didn't pay, and even when they did, they didn't cover costs. I took the whole gang. I'd rent two fifteen-passenger vans, get a bunch of hotel rooms, and blow some of my

Big Lake money on the experience. Much to our surprise, folks showed up to these road shows. People were actually watching our piece-of-shit show. We met them face-to-face. We looked them in the eye. I shook their hands. I hugged them. They'd thank me. I'd cut them off to thank them instead.

Our first road show was in Boston. The space was small, but we sold it out. A festival in North Carolina put us on their main stage, and our show got dark and disturbingly violent and caused a ton of walkouts. But you can't have walkouts if no one shows up to walk out in the first place! This thing was building. It was growing. We went back to Boston a year later and did a show that took place in the pool of a Holiday Inn. Halfway through, the managers of the hotel stormed the space and threatened to call the police on us. They were well within their rights. We were inciting chaos. Bananaman probably would have drowned in his costume if it hadn't stopped. I don't regret that we didn't finish it—the unplanned ending was perfect as it was. I didn't know it when we were driving up to Boston, but that show was always meant to conclude with an irate red-faced hotel manager screaming at us to stop.

In New York, though, the show audiences still felt empty at times. The comedy often failed. I kept a good head on my shoulders about it, but it's hard not to feel grim when an idea you believe in comes off as weak and disjointed and you don't realize it until it's being beamed out to the world. I didn't always love that the fans loved watching us screw up so much. If we screwed up less, they might grow to enjoy the things we were actually going for. For as much as I loved the show, I was still self-conscious about it.

Until the bands had our back.

Late-night TV used to show the world some of the best undiscovered bands and led to some amazing moments of television. Fear destroying the set of *SNL*. Elvis Costello getting banned from the same show. Billy Bragg calling out the Bush administration on Craig Ferguson. Music on late night has led to some of my favorite moments of chaotic television and I wanted to be a part of that lineage. We started reaching out to bands all over the tri-state area. Often we'd get quick rejections, or no answers at all. But the Brooklyn bands started catching wind that we were doing something interesting. I found a band called the Dolchnakov Brigade by googling the words "weirdest band in the world." Their songs revolved around "Palevish," a strange Nietzschean philosophy they'd made up for themselves. It was incomprehensible and involved them worshipping onions. They wore red leather bondage outfits and painted their faces. They appeared multiple times and became allies of ours.

When a band called Bad Credit No Credit played the show, they told me their parents were tuning in.

"Shit," I said. "Our show is so dumb. Your band is so good. Your parents deserve to see you on a real TV show."

"Hey," their lead singer, Carrie Anne Murphy, told me. "This *is* a real show. This is the only TV show we get to be on. Don't ever apologize for it again."

She reminded me of a core principle. No sorries. No caveats. No regrets.

When the So So Glos played our show, they told friends it was cool. They helped run an influential DIY space in Bushwick called Shea Stadium and word spread that our show was this weird fun thing to play. We became an outlier of the New York DIY scene, a thriving artistic community that we soon realized were kindred spirits. A pipeline had begun. The comedy scene in New York had initially bailed on us, but now this other wing of artists was starting to embrace us. We held shows at Death by Audio, one of the great DIY spaces in New York history. We'd do weird comedy and put together bills of bands that had all played our show. Our community of comedy nerds who didn't know music would come out, and the music community who didn't know comedy would show up, and our dorky comedy fans realized there were these other avenues to acceptance, other communities of rabble-rousers and weirdos. I felt immense joy, seeing that for some of these over- whelmed shy comedy kids I was bringing them into a DIY show for the first time, and they, too, would now get to worship at one of the altars that saved me.

As I aimed at success, I'd forgotten the lessons punk taught me. But I came back to the first community I ever knew that supported creativity for the sake of creativity and it kept me afloat even when my own comedy community didn't.

Our first public access episode aired on June 11, 2011. It wasn't until the end of October that we made a show I was actually proud of. And that was by accident. We'd been planning a Hal- loween show, with the aim of naming it our "Halloween Spook- tacular" to make fun of how often that dumb phrase is used.

My friend Connor Ratliff had been committing hard to a recurring bit on the show: he was running for president of the United States of America, and his platform consisted only of "I am thirty-five years old, and that's how old you have to be to run for president, so I guess I'm going to run for president." As part of this, he invited every presidential candidate onto our public access show to debate him. No one answered, except strangely enough Mitt Romney's campaign offered a very polite decline.

Weeks later, Connor got an email that simply said, "I'll do it." It was from Jimmy McMillan.

You may remember Jimmy McMillan as the "Rent Is Too Damn High" guy. He ran for public office a number of times back then. Mayor of New York. Governor. He would go for it, his entire plat- form being that rent in the city was too damn high. Connor had found his match: a mustachioed man who wore leather gloves and who, like Connor, also had a one-plank platform—"The rent is too damn high in New York City. Elect me president and I'll lower the rent so it won't be as damn high." McMillan was down to play ball and we were elated. But he was only able to do Halloween weekend. We said yes despite the fact that we'd already mapped out a whole plan for that week.

But in what I think was a pretty smart move, we "forgot" to cancel our Halloween show. Connor debated Jimmy surrounded by Halloween decorations. We didn't fill Jimmy McMillan in on any of what was happening—he told us he didn't want to know what we were up to and he'd figure it out on his feet. He rolled with the punches. I moderated a debate between Connor and McMillan, wearing a suit and trying desperately to keep a straight face. In the background sat dozens of oddball New York comedy and music fans in full Halloween garb. The set was decorated with orange and black lights, pumpkins, and big fake spiders as we spoke seriously about the goals of two loons who wanted to be president. McMillan wound up being brilliant. Connor never broke character. The whole thing became an hour-long self-contained performance art comedy piece, and when I walked offstage that night I realized that our show had finally hit a point where we pulled off a start-to-finish interesting hour of television. It was funny, it was fascinating, it was different. It was our show. It had taken twenty hour-long episodes that felt like pulling teeth to get there, but we'd done it. We'd taken the thing that existed somewhere in my head and heart and, because of a double booking, managed to broadcast exactly what I thought television could and should be.

Things started to break in March of 2012, when *New York* magazine published an article calling me the "Carson of Cable Access." Months later, the *New York Times* reviewed two talk shows on cable that aimed for a renegade feel, and then out of nowhere mentioned ours as an unscripted raw version of the same idea that was taking place on public access. Within a year we'd gone from a bizarre little show that comedy fans abandoned to a DIY artist haven getting a positive review in the most influential newspaper in the world.

The phone calls stopped being mean people lacing into us, confused people asking us what we were doing, or insomniac New Yorkers pranking us for their own amusement. We got calls from different states. It spread regionally and we could track it. Our first calls from New Jersey and Connecticut blew our mind. Then it reached the Midwest, the West Coast, and Fred called in from the middle of the Pacific Ocean. Canada. Puerto Rico. Brazil. Sweden. People were finding us. On Wednesdays people started dialing our number at nine o'clock, even though our show didn't go live until eleven.

Finally, at long last, meetings came. We were getting nibbles from actual cable networks. I spent hours preparing pitches. I knew how to explain the comedy of our show. I knew how to get excited about the interactive elements too. I knew the show backward and forward. And best of all I didn't care. I'd faced the industry before and let the pressure change me. Now I had an army at my back. An army of renegade filmmakers, and outsider comedians, and gnarly New York punks, and supporters from all over the world. Though I attended high-pressure meetings with industry bigwigs alone, before I walked through the door to face down some suit, I closed my eyes and imagined the faces of every single one of those people standing behind me, the real faces of the people I'd met in person and, behind them, the hundreds of faceless supporters and fans. I knew in my heart that if they knew this was happening, all those people would root me on for all the right reasons.

Development executives often had their own ideas, though. And they had nothing to do with the show. One network told me they *loved* the show so much—but could I make it focus on premiering new sci-fi and superhero movie trailers? I asked them point-blank how they loved the show if they wanted it to be an entirely different show. Before public access, I'd never have felt the strength to do that. But failure didn't scare me anymore. And I knew, even if I never made a cent from my public access show, that I had something pure. Another network said they wanted to buy the show outright. One small hitch: How would I feel about recasting the entire supporting ensemble? They felt like instead of using some of my real-life best friends on the show, it might make more sense for the cast to include a quirky Olivia Munn type. I have nothing against Olivia Munn, but I know that my friends and I spent years building something in the trenches together. It wouldn't work without all the people who contributed, and I wasn't going to ditch them now. Luckily, our mounting momentum and press regarding public access made me feel, for the first time in my career, that I could walk away.

Networks wanted to bastardize my thing. I didn't have to let them.

My time on public access allowed me to experience so many honest moments with so many people. Those moments are what the show has always been about. We did an episode where I registered as a real-life reverend, and three couples were married on our show. Three actual matrimonies in one episode of television! A lady once Skyped into the show from a hospital bed while already in the early stages of labor. How can you worry about the nervous concerns of corporate-minded executives when you have a show where people commit to lifelong love? You know what makes you feel impervious to the pressures that come with a pitch meeting? Knowing your show is a place where someone feels comfortable bringing life into the world.

A kid named Todd used to call into the public access show on a regular basis and became one of the many members of the community I knew as more than just a fan, but as someone who was a part of this network of humans the show helped support. Todd would always drop by the studio when visiting New York. Whenever I played Pittsburgh on the road, I'd reach out to Todd and we'd do our best to get together and say hi.

One night, Todd called the show and came out of the closet. My favorite part of this was that it wasn't a huge deal. It was our pal Todd. It was met with applause and warmth. It was a huge moment, but it also didn't matter, because it's 2018 and it shouldn't.

During a later conversation, Todd told me the way he told his mom about his identity was by playing her the clip of his call to our show. He said the show was the space that made him most comfortable sharing this information.

The show coalesced into being a safe harbor for people of all stripes to hang out, feel comfortable, and have some laughs. That started on public access, and every step of the way as things moved forward into more professional and higher pressure environments, I reminded myself of it. It's nice that the show became a job, but at the end of the day what it's always been about and always needed to be about was the people who watched it.

I took strength from those people. And anytime someone with an opportunity or some cash wanted to bastardize my show, I thought of them first. They gave me strength to fight tooth and nail to do things the right way.

In 2013, I booked a tiny part in *Anchorman 2*. (It was so small that it was initially cut from the movie and can now only be seen in the extended edition. That's classic Gethard right there.) I was reunited with my old champions, Will Ferrell and Adam McKay. My part was tiny and inconsequential; on set I mostly tried to just stay out of the way.

In between takes I lingered, as I often do, next to the craft-services table. This is the area on every television and movie set where you can grab free snacks, and very often this means at some point during the day a bowl full of peanut butter–filled pretzels will appear. Those bad boys move fast, so I was hovering, hoping to grab some if they showed up. Adam McKay sauntered up to the table.

"How ya been, Tic Tac?" he asked me.

"Not bad, sir," I said. "How about you?"

"Everything's good!" He smiled. "I'm loving your public access show."

"You watch that?" I said. I was stunned.

"Yeah, man, I'm a fan of yours. That's why I put you in a sitcom." He grinned. "I don't watch all the episodes, but I watch every clip you put online. That show is nuts. That show is you."

"Wow," I said. "Thanks for checking it out."

"When's that thing going to a network?" he asked me. "Who's producing it for you?"

"Nobody," I said. "I just kind of do it. No one wants to get on board."

"Really? That's nuts," he said. "I'll get on board. Can me and Will produce it?"

And just like that, Adam McKay and Will Ferrell became executive producers of my show. Not a show I would be attached to last minute. Not a show where we were all flying by the seat of our pants, seeing if it would even come to be. My show, that I built. All of this, mind you, because years prior I set aside a night to be a reader at an audition where I was never supposed to get any attention.

We shopped *The Chris Gethard Show* around. Someone actually bought it. You'll never guess who.

In 2014 we shot a pilot for Comedy Central. This felt like a full-circle victory. Four years after the sitcom flameout, I had another show in their pipeline produced by the same comedy badasses. Comedy Central, the same network that canceled *Big Lake*, wanted my show. They wanted me back.

We poured our hearts and souls into that pilot. I rented a gigantic house in the Catskills and brought the entire cast and crew there for a few days so we could all plan how to pull this thing off. Everyone was laser focused. We brainstormed, we cleared our schedules, we made sure that every single person involved in the show—from myself to the newest volunteers—was primed and ready.

Then, we fucked up. We listened too hard.

Comedy Central had no bad intentions. Their excitement was visceral. But they were asking us to do a ton of shit, and we were too scared to say no to them.

They wanted a new game in every act of the show. Acts are four to eight minutes long. This meant every time we came back from commercial, we had to explain a new game, take some calls, and play the game to its conclusion in five minutes or less. They wanted the Human Fish to live in a real pool. They wanted a character bit from Vacation Jason. They also wanted a celebrity guest and a musical act.

They wanted all this in twenty-two minutes.

We were used to having a full uninterrupted hour on public access. We now had half the time and they wanted four to five times the content we usually put into any given episode. Because we wanted to prove we were team players, we said "No problem" every time the network asked for something. In retrospect, we should have said, "If we want this to be great, we'll do about one-third of the stuff you're asking for and save the rest for later. Please trust us."

A month or so after filming our pilot, I was eating at a sandwich shop in Toronto by myself. I was out there for a week doing stand-up gigs. My phone rang. My manager's number popped up.

"Dude, you sitting down?"

I was about to get very good news or very bad news.

"Yeah," I said. "Give it to me quick. Like a Band-Aid."

"So the way they do these focus groups is they convince eighty random tourists in Las Vegas to come watch your show," he explained. "Then they ask them to give it a thumbs-up or thumbs-down."

"Got it," I said. "How'd we do?"

"Well"—he let out a sigh—"out of the eighty people who watched it, eighty gave it a thumbs-down."

"Wait," I said. "Did you say . . . you said eighty out of eighty? Every single one of them?"

"Yeah," he said. "The network really liked the show, but it was unanimous. One hundred percent of the people asked to give opinions on your show did not like it. They all loved Murf, but nothing else. I'm sorry."

I hung up the phone. I was in a foreign country, sitting by myself. I've never felt so alone.

I shit you not, at that moment, the song that was playing kicked into its chorus. It was "No One" by Alicia Keys, and I heard her repeating the phrase "Everything's going to be alright."

I knew Alicia was correct.

The Chris Gethard Show lives on. It refuses to die. I refuse to stop fighting for it. The punks and oddballs and film school rejects who found it and built it and made it their own still keep me going. In the face of failure and embarrassment, I almost gave up so many times. I'm so glad I didn't. Every one of the scars that have been left on this show as it got beat up and cast aside gave it character and life. I'm so proud of what it is. I'm so lucky to be a part of it.

But here's the thing: none of that matters.

Here's what matters—

When *The Chris Gethard Show* began at the UCB Theatre in 2009, I asked a band called the Kung Fu Monkeys to come play music for it. Their leader, James, was into it. His backing band was a bunch of local punk rock kids and they were the house band during our UCB days.

Just before we switched from the UCB version of the show to public access, James got a teaching job in Canada. He was out. Now I had a backing band with no leader. None of them had signed up to write songs.

Luckily, they were friends with a girl. She was a hell of a song-writer. She was also too busy to be a part of our dumb show—she had a background on Broadway, led her own band, and most recently starred in *De La Guarda* and *Fuerza Bruta*, two experimental aerialist dance theater shows that were legendary in New York.

Turns out, when you do high-flying aerial theater, there's a pretty big risk of getting injured. And this girl fucked up her back, bad. She couldn't carry groceries up her own steps. She couldn't perform in her shows anymore. She couldn't even strap her bass on to play with her own band.

So when the boys in my band reached out and asked her if she just wanted to sing with them and maybe shake some maracas from time to time, it couldn't have been more serendipitous. Her creative life was in jeopardy because of one bad accident. She was going nuts and needed an outlet to be creative after hers had been taken away. We'd built an environment full of people who were broken, and she fit the bill. (To be fair, most of us were broken emotionally, her ailments just happened to be physical.)

For the first year of our show, I was too nervous to talk to her. She was brilliant and talented and beautiful and brought so much to the table. Then in October of 2012, a bunch of us were out dancing in Brooklyn together. And everyone else went home.

She claims I leaned in and kissed her. This is a lie. She leaned in and kissed me.

Either way—her name is Hallie and now we're married.

That's what I got out of television. Screw the meetings, screw the money, the girls, the drugs. Screw the Hollywood roller coaster, screw all of it.

I walked into a public access station with a chip on my shoulder, wondering if I was making a huge mistake and sacrificing my entire career. It almost didn't work out. I still don't know if I built the career I wanted back then. But I now know I've built a life I never could have imagined for myself.

I walked into a public access station and I met my wife. She has my back harder than anyone ever has. She once had a dream that someone messed with me and she killed them with a fork. That's the most romantic thing I've ever heard.

All it took for us to meet was one bombed sitcom and a broken back.

I set out to find success and instead I found a family.

Thank God I remembered what really matters. Thank God for public access and thank God for broken people.

Thank God I failed.

RED LIGHT RULES

As you endeavor toward something—I don't care what field it's in—you're going to find experts who tell you how it "has" to be done. You're going to find YouTube tutorials, blogs with easy steps to success, books that claim to be guides to victory. Enjoy these resources, take what you can from them, and once you're done with them throw them all into the fire. Even this book. Examine every rule. Turn it over in your mind. Consider whether or not it works for you. If it does, keep it. If it doesn't, throw it out.

As you get closer to your dream, one of the most imperative steps is to build your own personal guidebook on how to go about doing things. Let this be defined by your experience, your instincts, your process of trial and error, and most of all by you and you alone. This doesn't mean you get to disregard anyone else's words or experience because you know better; it means considering every teacher's, guide's, and guru's words but ultimately showing some agency and deciding which of those sage words work best for you. Instead of simply using the tool kits they offer, you have to at some point build your own.

It is better to fail on your own terms than someone else's, so define those terms for yourself.

When it comes to my career, I always use "red light rules" as my guideline.

We all know what a red light means: Stop. Don't drive anymore. Take your foot off the gas, use the brake instead. That's what a light turning red means. That's what you have to do.

But you *don't* have to. If you really want to blow through a red light, you can. Physically speaking, your foot can remain on the gas if you so choose. There might be a shit storm of negative consequences, but you can risk it if you want to.

There are a million reasons why you should stop at a red light. Great ones. Chief among them: you might kill someone or yourself if you don't. You might be at a busy intersection where eighteen-wheelers full of heavy freight are whipping past, and the last thing you want is to take off your own head. You might collide with another car and take out a mailbox, getting you sued by both the other driver and the United States Postal Service. You might lose your license.

It's a very good idea to stop at red lights. It's a rule that I choose to opt into. We all should.

But . . .

Can you really say you've never sat at a desolate country intersection feeling a red glow on your face for way too long, wondering if the light itself is busted? How many minutes do you give it without another car passing by before you say "fuck it" and hit the accelerator? On a moonlit night when you can see there's not a car coming for miles in either direction, do you sit there forever? And if you do, don't you feel kind of like an asshole?

The rule doesn't make sense for us in that moment, so we choose to let it go. You run the red. Nothing bad happens. There's not a cop car hidden under fake bushes waiting to get you. In this case, no one would blame you for running the red light. It made sense to break a rule, and you took the time to note that it probably wasn't a huge deal to forgo it in that moment. The only consequences in that situation are positive; we waste less time and get where we're going sooner.

You can opt out of the things you are told you have to do if you take personal responsibility for doing so. Learning the rules is imperative. But part of knowing them backward and forward is knowing when you should break them.

For example, in comedy I'd say one of the main rules is "Do not enable hecklers." In fact, for most comedians the rule in this arena is probably closer to "You must eviscerate hecklers as soon as possible to stomp out their particular brand of awfulness."

There are a few types of hecklers. Some think their witty contributions help the show. This is never true. These hecklers can often be shut down with a few firm verbal smackdowns that let them know that you as a comedian can handle the room and their shouts aren't needed, thank you very much. Nine times out of ten, these people will get embarrassed in front of their dates, pipe down, and ultimately enjoy the laugh at their expense as the show moves on.

Most often, hecklers are people who enjoyed a few too many drinks. A lot of time they're alpha male bros who think beating a comedian verbally is going to help them get some tail later in the night. Any comedian with experience can shut down a drunk. You learn to be merciless and quick. It's best to put an end to things and move on. It's a point of pride knowing that I've eviscerated a heckler or two who has probably not hooked up that night because I embarrassed him. Hecklers shouldn't reproduce, and I've done my part.

Every once in a blue moon, a heckler is an actual lunatic. This presents a problem. Their perceptions don't match up with reality, so sometimes they won't go away even when their asses are handed to them.

One Tuesday back in 2014, I was doing a show called Hot Soup in the back room of an Irish bar on the Upper East Side of Manhattan. I was about to film a half-hour special and the booker offered me a slot to run my entire set. This was supernice of him; getting a full half hour of stage time in New York City is a rare luxury. It would be the last run-through of the material I'd do before heading up to Boston to film my first ever televised stand-up set. Needless to say, I was nervous. This show was the perfect environment. Bar shows have drunk crowds. That's not surprising. Humans plus booze equals drunk. Keeping their attention for a full half hour is an accomplishment. Plus, the Upper East Side isn't exactly a hipster hotbed. This wasn't going to be as easy a crowd as a room full of Brooklyn arts supporters would be for me. I wanted a tough room for my last practice round, and this one was perfect. I knew I'd have to work for it. I just didn't know how hard.

From the start of the show, an imposing man stood about four feet from the stage. Throughout every comic's set, he kept mumbling things. Customarily someone crammed that close to the stage would do their best to remain surreptitious. He went in the opposite direction, inserting himself into things in an odd, obtrusive way. The guy was tall, too, about six foot four. He was wearing a hoodie up to intentionally obscure his face. And he was chiming in in that way that was disruptive but not outright confrontational. It went on all night. Every comic had to deal with this hulking, mumbling, standing weirdo. Between his size and the fact that he was visibly insane, no one bothered to go after him. Sometimes when they're that nuts you just ignore it, then get bummed out that you traveled all the way to the Upper East Side for nothing.

He ruined the show. I was pissed. There was no way this was

going to be a productive rehearsal for my TV taping. On top of that, I knew that I was honor bound to abandon my set and go after the dude. I was the most veteran comic on the lineup, and I was closing. There's a code of honor in comedy, and sometimes the person headlining has to step up on behalf of the show. As a comedian I knew that I needed to hand this guy his ass if he tried his bullshit on me. Both for myself and the other comics who'd suffered through his nonsense before I took the mic.

Lucky for me, right at the beginning of my set he was handed a fresh bowl of French onion soup. We can all agree that French onion soup is by far the most disruptive type of soup. Most soups you can only make noise with. He took it to the next level, standing mere feet away, twirling long strands of mozzarella cheese around his spoon and loudly slurping broth. He'd switched from disruptive talking to obtrusive eating. I didn't want to get him for that. I needed him to come at me the way he'd been going the whole night. That way I could pin him to the wall in the most satisfactory fashion. I waited. At long last, he chimed in.

"Bust a nut," he said. I was about a third of the way through a story. I ignored it once. My story involved sex, but it certainly didn't warrant someone yelling a colloquialism for ejaculation that was most popular in the late 1990s.

"Bust a nut." I ignored it twice. I gave him one more chance and leaned harder into my material. Then about thirty seconds later, he said it again. "Bust a nut."

I turned and bared my claws, attack-mode style. In my mind, I was aiming to pin him to the ground like a jungle cat holding down his prey. I wanted to toy with this guy.

"Dude, everyone's been ignoring you all night," I said. "I'm not going to. What's your deal? Why do you need attention so bad? You've been disrupting the show from the start. This audience hates you."

This got murmurs of approval from the crowd. I'd done step one of the process: uniting myself and the crowd as allies in this cause. He would not have a chance to present himself as representative of their voice. Killing a heckler is a lot like chess.

"BUST A NUT," he yelled. This was an interesting counterstrategy, just yelling the same nonsensical phrase he'd been saying back at me, but louder.

"How does that apply here? Put your obsession with cumming on the back burner for a second. Stop. Just stop and talk to me. Don't say bust a nut again, it makes no sense. Can we just talk a minute?"

"Fine."

"Why are you doing this? What do you get out of it? You're just killing everyone else's good time."

"I feel like it."

"That's not good enough," I told him. "You can't do shit like this just because you feel like it. Everyone else in this room feels like punching you in the fucking face, but they know how to demonstrate basic restraint. Why do you think you have a right to do this?"

The crowd was even more on my side now. I heard a few scattered "Yeahs" and a bunch of grumbling and clapping. I hadn't attacked him comedically. I wasn't getting into a pissing contest with this lunatic. I could have gone after his appearance or his sloppy eating habits. That might tempt the crowd into seeing me as a bully though. Instead I tried to make it a public appeal, one where the crowd would get riled up. Over and over again, I wanted to underline that this guy messed up their night out on the town.

"I have a right to say whatever I want," the heckler told me.

"Why? That's not how life works."

"I can say whatever I want to you unfunny fucks," he told me. "I'm a comic too."

Rage took off like a rocket launch. It spread from my guts to my chest to my head. I knew I had him.

"You . . . you're not a comic," I said.

"Yes, I am, and I'm funnier than all of you," he said. "This has been a bullshit night of comedy."

"If you're really a comic," I said, "and you're behaving this way—"

"What?" He interrupted me.

"Then there is a special level of hell reserved just for you." The crowd cheered in approval. "You're not really a comic."

"Yes, I am!" he protested.

This is when I abandoned the rules. The rule in this situation is: shut down the heckler. You certainly don't ever look to *enable* them. But I had a lightbulb moment. It went against every muscle I'd trained as a stand-up, but I went with it. The red light philosophy went into action.

"Okay, look," I said. "If you're a comic, come up and prove it, motherfucker."

The crowd gave an "Ohhhh . . ." noise, as if they were about to see a fight. He stood up straight, confusion spreading across his face.

"What?" he asked.

"Do you really think you're funnier than me?"

"Yeah, I do," he said.

"I'm going to give you the microphone," I said. "Come up and do your set."

"Okay, but wait . . ." he said. He shook his head like he was trying to wake himself up. He needed to get psyched. He couldn't back down.

"If you're funnier than I am, no one will complain. The crowd will get a better show. I'll watch and learn."

"That's right, you will," he said.

"But I'm warning you—if you *aren't* as funny as me, after the way you've behaved tonight this crowd is going to *eat you alive*."

The crowd cheered. This back room of a bar on the Upper East Side was now the Roman Colosseum. He was backed into a corner. There's probably one thing that every comedian would agree upon when it comes to hecklers: you don't ever hand them the mic and walk offstage. But that's exactly what I did. I'd violated the number one rule of that situation. He never saw it coming, because I'd have to be more insane than him to do that. That was the one thing he hadn't counted on; that deep down I had the ability to be an even crazier fuck than he did. Now he knew he could either refuse and be branded a coward or accept and have to deliver. It was a no-win situation.

Checkmate.

He sauntered to the stage and grabbed the mic. He cleared his throat.

"Umm . . . hey," he said. The room went totally silent.

"So there's a . . ." He trailed off. "There's a guy . . . and you know that thing in New York City when you're, like, . . ." The crowd actually gave him a genuine shot. They sat with bated breath, waiting for this rambling setup to coalesce into some kind of routine. I lay in wait, praying that he didn't have an actual punch line, that he wasn't some undiscovered prodigy, the next George Carlin.

"That thing in New York City, where you fuckin' . . ."

There were a few shouts from the back. "You suck, bro!" "Garbage." And one very emphatic and perfectly enunciated "Fuck. You."

"You know what, fuck this," he said. He tried to put the mic back in the stand but couldn't figure out how. He bobbled it and cursed under his breath before placing the wire haphazardly in the holder and backing away from it, leaving the mic itself swinging and pointing toward the floor.

The wave of scorn that rolled from the back of that room to the stage was something I hope I never have to endure. If a crowd ever hates me that much, I will quit comedy forever. I know this did not happen, but in my mind the boos were so loud that they blew his hoodie off his head like wind. That's how forceful it was. He stepped back and put his arm up to block the lights, almost like they'd gotten brighter and attacked him.

He took a deep breath. He leaned toward the mic like he was going to say something.

"I . . ." His eyes went wide with panic. "I just . . ."

And then, he sprinted off the stage, out the door, and was never seen nor heard from again.

I'd been around the block with stand-up a fair number of times at that point. I wasn't some grizzled vet, but I was opening new doors and gaining momentum. I was confident that on some level I knew what I was doing. I knew the rules. I'd been in this situation before. I trusted my gut. So I broke the rules. It worked out.

In that case, the red light was "Don't hand that asshole the microphone."

And to further the analogy, handing him the mic was not just running the red light, it was putting my foot on the gas and closing my eyes as I approached the busiest intersection imaginable.

It could have been a disaster. It wasn't. Breaking the rule got me where I needed to go in the fastest, most brutal way possible.

Hitting the gas won't always work out. But it can. When you know the rules of what you're doing intimately, unquestionably, backward and forward and backward again, you can toy with them on rare occasions to great effect. Sometimes it will lead to catastrophe. You'll self-create a mess you have to clean up. But when ignoring, bending, or breaking a rule works out, it can be extremely rewarding. It can lead to innovation, to excitement, to undiscovered territory that helps you claim ownership of your craft.

Even in the busiest intersections, sometimes none of the bad stuff will happen if you ignore the red light and keep driving. You'll dodge the truck. The mailbox will be fine. You'll look like a madman, but also feel really fucking cool, like you're in a '70s cop thriller with a badass car chase.

I challenge you to break a rule in your pursuit once in a while, even when you're pretty sure it will create a headache for you. Learning how to handle these headaches, sort them out, and recover from them is possible. On top of that, strengthening the muscle of taking risks is an asset. Failures that come from risk taking have the potential to yield some of the highest rewards. It only takes one stab at greatness to work out. Going off the grid and doing something outside of the traditional methods or expert advice might just be what makes the dam break for you.

It's foolish to put yourself in danger. It's irresponsible to imperil innocent passersby. But if it ends well and it gets you to a goal? More power to you. Because you took the power for yourself. Taking that power once in a while, whether it leads to success or failure, is one of the most necessary steps you have to take. If you never learn to do that, then all the stories you hear about dreams being impossible might as well be true.

THE UNUSUAL THINGS

Your experiences add up to the life you live.

When you sit around with friends, you don't tell stories about normal days. When your college pals reunite, stories don't start with sentences like, "Remember all those days we went to class, came home, studied, watched half of a movie and fell asleep around eleven?"

You tell the stories of the time your roommate pushed a couch out of a second-floor window. You reminisce about the party that got so out of control the cops showed up. You talk about the professor who lost his mind and rambled about conspiracy theories.

When you're with family, you talk about the disaster fiftieth wedding anniversary party where someone got too drunk and did an impromptu a cappella performance of "Somewhere Over the Rainbow." When you run into someone you used to work with, you don't opine over how nice the cubicles were; you compare notes on all the rumored scandals and secret office romances. When you tell a tale of a vacation you went on, you never say "Yeah and then we stopped at a great gas station before crashing at a nondescript Red Roof Inn." You talk about the outlandish stuff. You talk about the unexpected stuff.

It's the unusual things, the disruptions, that we focus on when we think about the best moments from our life.

Make an active effort to live a life filled with those moments.

FUNNY PLUS

Once you reach some level of proficiency, what do you do next? If by some miracle you dip your toes into the world of creating and actually feel comfortable with how it turns out, what happens then?

Well, first, you do it a thousand more times. You outwork the next person. You put in the time, you grind it out, you practice your scales. The terror didn't intimidate you. So you have to do it enough times that you invite the terror back in, so you can face it down again. You find out if this instinct and urge to create is a passing interest, a fantasy, or maybe somehow against all odds is an actual passion that's going to burn over time.

If it is something that doesn't feel like it's going to stick, that's perfect. Congratulations. You can walk away with your head held high through that miraculous place where you realize that you've pursued your dream to completion, or at least to a point of completion you can live with. That seems like such a healthy, happy place to end up. Amazing.

But if you are compelled to keep going, you'll reach new tiers of proficiency every so often. Sometimes you'll go on hot streaks where your skills will take leaps, your ideas will flow freely, and your methods of getting them out to the world will deliver them to people.

But more often than not, these steps will spread out further and take more time. The initial progress moves quickly, because there's so much room to grow. And then you'll spend years plateauing, which will start to feel a lot like desperation. The awareness that you're no longer developing is often worse than the initial frustration you felt when you were trying to get started.

Then, you'll take another step. Then another, consistently and determinedly, for your duration as an artist.

At some point, you'll realize you're actually pretty good at what you do.

And here's where I'll put a personal challenge out there to you. Something that assumes you don't fail, which is counter to most of what I've championed in this book. I've been bracing you for failure, encouraging it and celebrating it. So here is a challenge should you stumble your way into success:

Give them something more.

Don't settle for proficient. Don't settle for good. Don't even aim for greatness. Aim for uniqueness. Try to put something in your work that marks it as your own. Have a calling card. Make stuff in such a way that people will immediately know it's yours.

When I hear the first few bars of a Jawbreaker song, I know it's theirs. Not just because I'm a huge fan, but because their sound is their sound. It only takes a few seconds. I get transported to the world they built because they have a signature feel.

When I see a Jack Kirby drawing, I don't need to check the byline to know who drew it. His comics exploded for a reason. Marvel took over the world of comics once Jack Kirby let loose with his art. Part of the company's success was because the characters were written with foibles and vulnerability. But part of it was because Jack Kirby's art hit a level where it was unmistakably his. There was a tone, a foundation, a visual invitation into those comic books that infected all of Marvel's earliest work.

Find out if you can do it. Then do it. Then do it *your way.*

In my opinion, leaving your mark in the field that you love is the only true indicator of success, much more than money, fame, or attention.

For the last decade, I've worked with this challenge in mind, and while it's made my life more difficult it has served me very well. The first seven years of doing comedy was just about getting halfway decent. After a year or two, I started to think I was pretty great until I realized I was actually hot garbage. Sometime around 2004, I thought I'd gotten pretty good, but I was still only okay. By 2007 I took a deep breath and realized—*yeah, I'm at least somewhat good at this. But now what?*

So for the past ten years I've given myself a mantra. I've never shared it with the world. It's goofy, and a little embarrassing. There's a two-word phrase I always mumble to myself when I'm writing, strategizing my next steps, or thinking big—"Funny plus."

At some point I thought about my heroes, the people who inspired me to do comedy in the first place. I realized what they all shared in common was that they weren't *just* funny. The long-lasting influences that have stood the test of time had an extra level on top of the laughs that's stuck with me.

For example, most people don't know that my first comedic love was Eddie Murphy. I was born in 1980, and I bet most guys of my age will say that *Coming to America* was absolutely the funniest movie of our era. *Caddyshack* and *Animal House* were for kids slightly older than us. *Coming to America* was our shit. I became obsessed with Eddie Murphy. I loved everything he did on *SNL*—Gumby and Stevie Wonder and "I Hate White People."

Eddie Murphy was *so funny.* But I don't point to him as an

influence anymore. He was wickedly hilarious, bomb-droppingly funny, but it hasn't stuck in my gut as much as some others. (It probably doesn't help that his two specials have some stuff that was sadly okay back then but has aged into coming off as hateful in the time since.) Eddie was funnier than anyone. Why hasn't that lingered in my psyche as much as the work of some others who weren't as hilarious as him?

Letterman stuck with me. I believe it's because when Letterman was at his best, he wasn't just funny. He was funny *and* subversive. He was poking holes in the rules. That was the stuff I loved the most, that created an obsession that became for me not just appreciative of laughs, but analytical of its intent.

I don't morally endorse a lot of what Howard Stern did in his early days. It hasn't aged well. I think he'd probably admit that even while being proud of his body of work and his legacy. But growing up in the Northeast in the '80s and '90s, Howard was inescapable and we all loved him. He was broadcast on the airwaves. My bus driver used to play his show on the way to school. (Inappropriate!) When I listen back now, the stuff I love the most about his old days isn't him making naked ladies ride a sex toy or his exploiting the alcoholism of a dwarf. The secret to Howard Stern, in my opinion, is that he was funny *and* familial. You didn't come back for the stunts. The stunts tricked you into listening in the first place. "Did you hear what Howard did this morning?!"

What you came back for was that you heard so genuinely that Howard really cares about Robin. That he really thinks Fred is weird. That Gary was pissing him off that week, that Artie was annoying him, that Jackie and Ronnie the Limo Driver were mad at each other over something dumb. It sounded like friends, it sounded like family, and it felt like a reality show before reality shows were a thing. The reason to roll your eyes at Howard is a lot of the bits. The reason to love Howard is that he built a world of real cares and connections between people, and he invited us, his listeners, in.

The master of adding extra layers was Andy Kaufman. I always cite him as my favorite comedian and my biggest influence. He's the person whose work inspires me to be at my best with my own. This is paradoxical to some people. The most popular things I've done are *Career Suicide, Beautiful/Anonymous,* and *The Chris Gethard Show.* Each of those is renowned for an unusual level of honesty, where I wear my heart on my sleeve. Andy was known for bending reality, committing to characters to a dangerous degree, and never revealing his true self. This feels like it couldn't be more opposite of the things I've done.

But here's what I continue to love about Andy Kaufman and be so impressed by: he never settled for funny. His work was, in my opinion, *always* funny. But that was never his point. This demonstrates to me a supreme confidence in himself that he was funny. He didn't need to think about that part. It was the base level, the foundation. When he got onstage at comedy clubs, he probably found that confidence because he knew at a base level that he was a goofball silly guy who could make people giggle.

But all his bits have a remarkable layering. He pushes it so far in so many directions that it makes it impossible all these decades later to define him as an artist. Most commonly, his work was hilarious but also infuriating. Wrestling women. Tony Clifton. These were things he did where people wound up legitimately furious, but simultaneously laughed. That's not an easy thing to do. Getting slapped by Jerry Lawler on Letterman was funny but terrifying. His Carnegie Hall concert, which ended with the Rockettes and Santa Claus storming the stage before Andy took the whole audience out to get milk and cookies, was funny and ecstasy inducing.

His comedy was comedy but was always something else, too. It was challenging, for himself and the audience. It probably ruined his career and maybe his life. I admire it so much.

Which is why for the past ten years I've worked under the challenge of "funny plus." When I do things the world hears about, I want them to have a layer on top of them. Here's how my methodology goes.

I do tons of stand-up. This makes me confident I'm still funny. There is no way to know you're funny except to prove it. I go up on stages in New York City. I go to clubs, and different types of clubs. I go to the Comedy Cellar, where the legendary reputation of the club means the audiences have impeccably high standards. You have to be funny to get laughs in that room. I go to the Stand, where the crowds are New Yorkers, Jersey and Long Island people, locals. They tend to be a little rowdy, a little working class. I go to other clubs where the crowds are mostly German and Australian tourists. (From what I can tell, Australians vacation nine months a year.) I go to North Brooklyn, to artsy rooms where you can take your time and have fewer punch lines, but you'd better be thoughtful and innovative. You need to take risks and be punk rock there. I go to South Brooklyn, where you're in front of discerning and appreciative crowds, people who subscribe to *The New Yorker* and listen to NPR. I do colleges. I do rock clubs. I do festivals. I aim to play these jokes in front of people of every demographic. Every age. Every gender. Every race. Every class. Every creed.

If I can get a joke or story to work for all those crowds, I know it is a good joke. If it gets laughs, I'm funny. If it gets laughs in all those locations, the joke is good. I don't consider a joke good unless it is universal, and to know whether or not it's universal you need to put it in front of everyone. And if it doesn't work for one of those groups, I don't consider it my A material, and I don't plan on ever putting it out on a special or album. Only the things that work *everywhere*. This is why I work for years on each individual joke.

But that, when I am at my best, is my *starting point*.

With *The Chris Gethard Show*, anyone who's seen it knows that I want it to be funny but that it's also absurd and escapist and confusing and strange. This is intentional. But if I'm being honest, those aren't my priorities. Letterman nailed all those things, and my chasing of them is reflective of how often I rip him off. (There are no original ideas, so I aim to rip off the best.) For *TCGS*, my secret aim has always been to make something funny and *inclusive*. When I started the show at the UCB Theatre, it was ultimately my twisted personal rip-off of Letterman. When I brought it to public access, though, the phone calls made my eyes light up. I saw an opportunity to involve people more than other television shows had before. I wanted to put viewers in the show itself, to make it a shared exchange between me and the audience, and to build a community surrounding the project. Funny. Yes. Top priority. But secondary layer? Include the people who support it directly in the show itself.

Career Suicide was an effort to be funny and *brutally honest*. But it was also my effort to be funny and, for the first time in my career, to *attack*. My ultimate goal with that show was to say things that I felt weren't said to me when I was fifteen years old, and twenty-two years old, and at every other point that I was at my most depressed and unhealthy. I wanted to put on record some things that were simple, and human, and honest that I thought might destigmatize some issues that affected me and many others. I had a mission statement in my head. Maybe people younger than me who suffer in the same ways I do might have some helpful ideas placed in the ether in a way I didn't if I could push it far enough. And I pushed it to HBO. I'm proud of that.

Most of all, the thing I'm proudest of is that *Career Suicide* wound up being both funny and *illuminating*. Because while many people who suffer from mental illness have reached out with kind words about the piece and its effect on them—and that means the world to me, truly—there is another group who've written to me that means even more. I've had countless messages from people who *don't* suffer, but who see it from the outside looking in. They tell me that because of *Career Suicide*, they understand mental illness just slightly better now. That's everything to me. People have said they now better understand their kids, their parents, their significant others—people who are in the thick of it—who are scared and unable to explain their heads while they're in it. My show about my own brutal experience with having a crazy sad brain and being honest after the fact helped. It showed people who have never been there how a thing that is unexplainable feels. It will probably stand as the thing I'm most proud of at the end of my life.

Beautiful/Anonymous was an effort to be funny and *selfless*. As an improvisor, you learn to put the other actor on a pedestal and honor their idea before your own. If I'm working hard to make you look brilliant, and you're working to make me look brilliant, then we both look brilliant. It doesn't always go that way, but that's the technique and philosophy, improv's ultimate goal. I wanted to do that with people who aren't improvisors and don't realize that my training exists while they're interacting with me. While on the phone with strangers, I look to put them on a pedestal, say yes to their ideas, find the unusual aspects of what they're saying, and to help them heighten the most interesting aspects of what they're creating. These are all tried-and-true techniques of basic improv. I want to be the straight man to anyone in the world via the phones with that project.

That one doesn't always hit the mark, because many of the best episodes aren't funny. The episodes get serious, thoughtful, and *sometimes* funny. This can drive me a little batty at times, but I've had to once again learn to let the ego go. The project is beloved by many and I've learned to embrace it as the most mature work I've done, which makes sense, because I'm no longer a young buck. Because *Beautiful/Anonymous* is so small, so personal, and so intimate, I've learned to love it as a private getaway from the pressures of the rest of my career and I remain fiercely devoted to it.

The book you are holding—I hope you laugh many times while reading certain parts of it. But what I hope is clear is that I also want it to be encouraging, full of tough love, empathetic, and hopeful.

I pray that the above stretch doesn't come off too much like I'm patting myself on the back. I only want to hold up my own choices as examples, which I hope shows that I put my money where my mouth is, so to speak.

I don't brag, because I'm not sure all the above efforts were even successful. *The Chris Gethard Show* has tons of haters and is in constant peril of getting canceled. Every time an episode airs I get hateful tweets. I get kind ones, too, don't get me wrong, but the hate is there. As mentioned, *Beautiful/Anonymous* veered off the comedy track so far that it frightened me and I had to give over into acceptance. I had to let it be what it is, not what my insecurities wanted it to be. And with *Career Suicide*, many pure comedy fans hated it. They say I prioritized emotions and issues over jokes. That I skipped the line on getting a special on HBO—a high-water mark for any comedian—by speaking about social ills but without strong enough punch lines.

I don't know if any of these people are right or wrong. But I *do* know, always, that I'm proud of the chances I've taken and can rest easy knowing how hard I work. I make things. I try to make them good. And on top of it all, I put in a lot of effort to leave my fingerprints on them.

When you learn to walk, you might learn to run. When you learn to run, you might even learn someday how to run fast. And, at that point, I hope you find a way to leave a tiny impact on the world that's all your own. Do so by taking it to the next level, and someplace unexpected. When you realize you've learned how to run fast, it's your responsibility to make the types of choices that could cause you to trip and fall at top speed. These are the layers no one will see coming. These are the layers only you can add. These are the moves that reflect that you haven't settled and never will. This is the strategy that offers the dim hope that you won't be remembered as one of a mass of proficient people, but rather as one of the few brave outliers who weren't okay with simple validation and instead aimed to leave an actual mark.

Your work will stand out as unique and, in my opinion, more noble, because you risked failing instead of settling for an easy win. Only a minuscule percentage of people who set out to climb a mountain will actually make it to the top. Should you somehow be one of them, I challenge you to actually do something once you reach the peak.

ALWAYS BE TERRIFIED

If success does manage to come your way, congratulations. You are one of the lucky few. But then a funny thing happens: the challenges that seem insurmountable right now will come to feel easy. You'll get to the mountaintop, put your dream into action . . . and then it will become a fact of your life. It will no longer seem hard.

If all your dreams come true, that's the best-case scenario—that you manage to conquer the unconquerable until it becomes commonplace.

The duty of any creative soul is to avoid the sad fate of complacency. When you get to a point of proficiency, where your dreams don't terrify you anymore, I highly encourage you to find that terror anew in some other area of life. You should make it a lifelong goal to *always be terrified.*

Find the next challenge. Seek out the environment where you're in over your head. Remember—one of your main goals is to learn to coexist with the terror of failure. You'll learn to love failure. Even when you're not failing at your primary goal, find ways to share your life with failure so that it never seems daunting again.

In my early days at the Upright Citizens Brigade Theatre, I liked to show up hours before a show. I'd get hyped up backstage like I was a professional athlete. I'd run warm-up exercises with my teams. I'd get onstage hungry, excited, and terrified that it wasn't going to go well. It was like walking on a high wire.

By 2012, I was twelve years in as a performer at that theater. I started arriving minutes before showtime. I'd check my phone while walking backstage on the way to my entrance. It wasn't scary anymore. I was skilled. I was practiced. It was still a high wire, but a high wire I'd walked thousands of times before. I was ninety-nine percent certain before I stepped on the stage that I wasn't going to fall off the high wire.

So I quit.

I have no room for complacency in my life, so I switched to stand-up. It was brutal, humbling, and unpredictable. It reminded me of the old days, when I was twenty years old and taking a train into the city to do improv shows and getting on a stage still felt like the most insane thing in the world to me. I put in years getting good. Failing onstage alone stings a lot more than being up there with a group. At least with improv you can all go to the bar and commiserate after a shitty show. With stand-up, you feel like you got pinned and mounted to the wall. Bombing at stand-up feels like a public execution.

But after many moons of bombing and going back up, I figured out my voice in that medium as well. It started to feel easier. I was learning to conquer it.

So I reupped the challenge. I sought out the least friendly environments: road shows, clubs where longer stories from a sensitive emo guy usually don't fly, spots with drunken and aggressive crowds. I got dinged up and intimidated and knocked around . . . but I learned to love that as well. Going into hostile rooms at first felt like walking into a Wild West saloon where anyone might pull a gun. I eventually learned to enjoy that thrill. After a while I learned to do it well on a consistent basis, and part of the fun of stand-up became knowing that I didn't just need good jokes, I needed to be able to take the temperature of a crowd within a few seconds of taking the stage. That got a little comfortable . . .

So I auditioned at the Comedy Cellar. This is the best comedy club in the world. Comics don't allow themselves to bomb there. You bring your A game. The night I auditioned was one of the scariest of my life. I filmed my HBO special a few months before auditioning at the Cellar and can honestly say that the Cellar audition was more terrifying.

I entered the club and was told I'd be doing five minutes following Ray Romano. I watched his set. A loving crowd embraced him, overjoyed to see the guy they knew and loved from television. He could have just soaked it all up and phoned it in that night, but instead he murdered. His jokes were on point, and he demonstrated a veteran's level of comfort and skill. His jokes were so sharp they would have crushed that set if he wasn't Ray Romano, but he was. He got a standing ovation on his way offstage.

Then I shambled up there. My first joke was told over the mumbles of the crowd, who were still processing that they'd seen one of their favorite sitcom stars in the flesh. The first half of my joke quieted the hubbub, but just barely. The second half built up to the punch line and the excited, unruly masses finally quieted down. I'd picked my most dependable jokes, and I hit my first real punch line. There were a few chuckles, but nothing to write home about. Deep in my performer's brain, a red flag was rising, and all this was going down while the club's booker was watching.

After my first joke, a woman in the front row said just loud enough for the whole room to hear it, "Huh. That was actually kind of funny."

"See, people?" I said. "Ray Romano gets a standing ovation.

That's great for him. That's not what I want, though. I want to tell
you a joke and have one audience member quietly reassure me that
I am funny."

This self-awareness got the crowd on my side and they were with
me. I got passed at the Comedy Cellar, which sounds like a bad
thing. It's not. To get passed means you're invited to perform there
on a regular basis. I go up there a few nights a week now and just
try to keep up with all the amazing comics on their stage. Someday
that will feel like a safe environment for me. It will get easier. When
that day comes, I know it's on me to find a new terror.

The terror in your life doesn't need to come solely from advanc-
ing at your craft. Sometimes I do like letting comedy be fun. I
don't need comedy to beat the shit out of me on a daily basis, just
in the times when the challenge has plateaued.

So to make sure I *am* getting the shit beat out of me I take Brazilian jiu-jitsu classes at the Renzo Gracie Academy. Many regard
this as the top jiu-jitsu school in the world. I do not belong there.
It's filled with professional athletes, aspiring mixed martial arts
fighters, and former Division I wrestlers. At the end of each class,
you participate in a series of live sparring rounds, wrestling classmates to see who can tap out the other first using chokes or joint
locks. I wound up paired with a 135-pound woman who proceeded
to destroy me. During our 6-minute-long round she tapped me at
least a dozen times. Every time I tried to even grab on to her, she
used my own momentum to put me in a bad position. I'd lunge
forward and wind up face-planted on the mat. I'd try to get around
to her back and she'd somehow wind up on mine, locking me in
a lightning-fast choke hold. When the round mercifully ended, I
was shell-shocked. I felt like I'd just tried to fight wind. A class-
mate saw the dazed look on my face and asked me if I was okay.

"Yeah," I said. "I'm good. But, Jesus, that blond girl beat the hell
out of me."

"Of course she did," he said. "She fought in the UFC three nights ago."

There's no world in which it makes sense for me to be in a grappling match with someone rising in the ranks of the planet's greatest fighting organization. I tell jokes for a living and have a degenerative joint condition. It's not logical for me to dedicate so much time to jiu-jitsu. I'll never be great at it.

And that's why I love it. It means I won't go through a week without feeling defeat. Comedy used to demoralize me on a near daily basis. Now I only bomb and question everything once or twice a month. So I've refilled the tank of terror with something entirely unrelated to my field. It's on you to do the same.

Right now, at the beginning of this journey, you should be terrified. If you're taking your own goals seriously and you're not terrified, something's probably wrong. Being terrified is a good thing even though it doesn't feel like it. I know that you want nothing more than for that terror to go away. It will someday.

But when it does, do the hard thing and challenge yourself. Never rest on your laurels. There's always another level to reach. There's always another environment you can conquer. When the terror becomes too exhausting and you just don't want to deal with it anymore, you've probably earned your retirement. When that day comes, you can sail into the sunset and be proud of what you've accomplished.

But before that time comes, I'm sorry to tell you that if you're not terrified, you're not challenging yourself. Put in the work and see where you can really take this thing.

If you're not feeling scared, you're not growing. If there's no room to grow, then there's no room to breathe. Things that can't breathe die, even ambitions.

PUSHING THROUGH BLOCKS

Blocks are coming. And they'll be nasty when they get here.

You'll find yourself sitting in front of a blank canvas, brushes prepped, paints mixed. You'll go to make that first mark and you'll freeze. You'll spend hours in front of a computer monitor, typing a sentence then erasing it. You'll know you're stalling out. You'll have all your materials bought. Your tools will be sharpened. You'll give them a disinterested shrug that makes you feel totally hopeless and mad at yourself. The canvas will remain blank.

Conquering a creative block can be one of the most victorious feelings. When you've sat and scratched your head for hours, refreshing social media, burning away the work hours, then you get that first paragraph going only to have the rest of your piece tumble effortlessly out of your fingers? That feeling is as good as any other I know. It's like the end of a bad constipation. (As someone who often suffers from both, I have long debated whether creative or bowel constipation is more frustrating.)

I don't want to rob you of those moments where the dam breaks and the ideas come pouring forth. There are stretches where such incidents are all we have to keep us going. Fight, tooth and nail. Get through those blocks. The accompanying adrenaline rush is a well-deserved reward, and a great motivator to get back to work the next day. There are many days where you're going to carve out eight hours of your time to pursuing your goal and the first seven hours are going to be a distracted, worthless shit show, the opposite of productive. You have to have those. That last hour might be the most productive burst of the whole project. We have those seven awful hours of frustration and self-directed anger to get to that one badass sixty minutes of creation.

But...

There are other days where the eighth hour sucks too. There are times where you stand up and realize you wasted a day of your life and got no closer to your goal. Our lack of momentum feels like we're stalling out on the side of a highway. When we stand still, it can make it feel like our dreams are racing away from us, leaving us in their dust.

On those days, you'll often feel some variation of "This whole thing is worthless. My time would have been better spent doing *anything else.*"

This was a huge issue with me for many years. I'd have days spent banging my head against the wall, wondering why I couldn't focus and get a simple to-do list done. Those days were followed by nights of restless sleep. And the next day, I'd approach my computer with the same attitude I'd have around a venomous snake. The tool of my trade came to trigger all the self-doubts I had about not being in the trade itself. It's a nasty cycle.

This happens for people of all stripes with all sorts of goals. We all know the shame that comes with putting on workout clothes, then finding excuses to not leave the house. "I just have to answer that one email. Oh, shoot, I got a Facebook notification . . ." Next thing you know it's six hours later and you're sadly slinking out of your athletic shorts never having gone to the gym. A lot of key-boards set up in corners by people who want to play piano turn into de facto storage spaces and secondary coffee tables. Unused tools and unused ambitions can clutter our homes and our heads.

So on those days when it feels like the time you've set aside for chasing your goal would be better spent doing anything else, my advice to you is—do anything else.

Anything.

Go see a movie. Walk around the park. Call a bunch of college friends you haven't caught up with in a while. Do whatever strikes your fancy, as long as it doesn't involve sitting around feeling frustrated and, eventually, angry at yourself.

My loving shrink of ten years handed me another gem, which I am grateful for since it came in exchange for my hard-earned cash. She saw the level of stress I was under trying to wrangle my demons. She noted how unproductive this behavior was.

She laid it out bluntly: Some days you just don't have it. Maybe instead of sitting in a bubble of frustration, go out into the real world. Real life might hand you inspiration.

Again, fight the good fight. I don't want anyone using this chapter as an excuse to fuck off from real responsibility and go to the movies just for the sake of it.

But the next time you find yourself creatively blocked, I invite you to look in a mirror. Say the following out loud: "Do I have it?"

If the answer is "Not right now," follow it up with this question: "Is it because I'm fucking around?"

If the answer is yes, and you can admit to yourself that you're spending too much time getting willingly distracted, tell yourself the following: "Well, cut that shit out."

Then go get back to work.

But if the answer is an honest "No, I'm really not fucking around. I'm focused, I've got time carved out for this, my phone ringer is turned off, and my sister is watching the kids. I've done everything I can to position myself for productivity, the well has just run dry today," at that point you need to flee the scene of the crime.

Go out into the real world. Experience stuff. Consider it research for the next day's valiant effort. Maybe, just maybe, you'll encounter something so worth singing about, drawing about, writing about that it will inspire you and obliterate the roadblocks.

Creative blocks happen when we get inside our own heads and point everything inward. Placing our focus outward, into the real world, can often help us survive.

THE CURRENT STATE
OF THINGS

After many years of tumult, my life has settled into something I'm happy with.

My wife has my back. We own a little co-op apartment in Queens. There's a garden for the residents of the building. There's a laundry room in the basement, but the machines are often out of order. It's fine. My small life is nice.

Hallie recently had another dream where someone messed with me. In the dream she looked for her fork but couldn't find it, so she used her thumbs to take out their eyes. I swooned when she told me.

Professionally things are going better than ever, which is why people ask me for advice in the first place. I have three main sources of income. You may be surprised about which is my favorite.

First, there is my pride and joy, *The Chris Gethard Show*. Every day I get to work on the show is a blessing. I met my wife through the show. Two other couples got married after meeting via the show. One of them has a baby. *A human life came into existence because of this show*. It has deep meaning to me and always will.

Around seventy people have jobs through the show, another point of pride for me, but also a tremendous source of stress. Although working on my own television show—where we take chances, mess with the expectations of viewers, and try to shatter the conventions of television itself—is my dream, it requires a lot of hard work, long hours, and a lot of energy. It beats me up. It exhausts me. I wouldn't trade it for anything in the world. But due to the never-ending fear of letting everyone down, it's not my favorite source of income.

The second leg of my career tripod is my podcast, *Beautiful/ Anonymous*. I couldn't be more fortunate to have stumbled into this simple, strange idea, which has been embraced by a separate audience from the rest of my work. Every week I get on the phone with a random anonymous stranger. I tweet out a number. Thousands of people attempt to call in. The record for call attempts stands at over fourteen thousand dials off one measly tweet. I randomly select one caller from that barrage of phone calls. It's like playing the lottery, only you win heartfelt conversations between strangers instead of money. An anonymous human on the other end of the line tells me about their life. I'm not allowed to hang up for an hour. Sometimes the calls are funny. Just as often, they're dark. The callers come from all walks of life. They have hopes, victories, failures, and dreams like everyone else. I'm proud to provide a platform where people can air out their concerns and their stories. The veil of anonymity makes people feel comfortable. I get to be a facilitator for people to put the stories of their lives on record. I'm not center stage on the podcast, real people are. I love it so much.

Like most of my projects, no one quite believed in *Beautiful/ Anonymous* when it began. I'm aware that the premise sounds a little boring. A single phone call with an unknown, unvetted stranger. I wanted regular Joes and Janes. No one of note. The average people you pass on the street every day. The person on the subway. The lady who stole your parking spot. What are their stories? Real life, if you ask me, is the most interesting thing in the world.

It worked. The first time I tweeted out that phone number, hundreds of calls poured in.

For a few weeks it was the number one downloaded podcast in the world. It instantly became more popular than anything I've ever done and I was overwhelmed with the response and the kindness. I still am. Any time I get to sit in that booth, put on headphones, and shut out the entire world besides the one person I'm talking to, I feel like the luckiest person on Earth.

But a funny thing has happened along the way: the podcast isn't comedy. It is, at the end of the day, about the people who call. It turns out that they aren't interested in this platform being used for comedy. I'm fine with that. To be completely honest, I kind of love it. People have used the show to tell me about escaping from cults. About being married to someone and finding out their partner is into child pornography. About what it's like to navigate the world as a deaf person. The show often gets heavy, but it's always full of empathy. I love it.

But the lack of comedy means that ultimately, even the laidback and welcomed conversations of *Beautiful/Anonymous* aren't my favorite peg in my career. I'm a comedian at heart and need to maintain that.

That's why stand-up trumps all.

I'm lucky to get out on the road these days. I play colleges, rock clubs, and any other strange road gig that will have me. The travel is brutal—early mornings and late nights, time away from my wife. The only way I've managed to enjoy it is to become addicted to accruing frequent-flier miles. (When up-and-comer comedians catch some momentum and ask me for advice, the first words out of my mouth are "You never fly without being signed up for that airline's frequent-flier program. If you do, you're a fool!")

But stand-up makes me feel free. It's the ultimate in self-determination. If I can make people laugh and if I can sell some tickets doing it, that's enough. That gives me a right to do it. Then I get to say what I want up there onstage. If it hits, I get to make people happy. I get to do it on my own terms. What an amazing gig.

It's the most terrifying thing too. When you bomb at stand-up, that means a whole room of people don't like you. They don't like what you said. They don't like how you chose to say it. They don't enjoy you, as a human or as an artist.

The gigs can be miserable. There are no happy endings that erase occasional shame and misery. No matter how experienced you get, you will always bomb once in a while. You might have a dozen amazing sets in a row. It doesn't matter. Any of them could be endlessly painful, and every time you step onstage could be it. I once got to a college and was told I had to set up my own lights. The crowd was already loaded in and watched me and the other comics try not to electrocute ourselves.

I did another college show at five in the afternoon in the basement of an empty campus library. Every few minutes a PA would come to life. "Twenty minutes until the library's closing." Five minutes later: "Fifteen minutes until the library's closing." A lot of succeeding at stand-up is about momentum and rhythm, and it's hard to find those things when an angry librarian is shouting at you through a blown-out speaker. There were only a handful of attendees, and while I'm not arrogant, the show was in my home state of New Jersey and I was on *Broad City* at the time. I should have at least filled half that room on a college campus. Later, I found out the college had scheduled another comedy show that same night, much more heavily advertised, featuring Dave Coulier. Nobody can compete with fucking Uncle Joey.

But when standing on a stage and rambling into a microphone

goes right, there's nothing like it. I feel drunk on adrenaline. I feel energized and powerful and like I've somehow superseded every one of my many, many insecurities. Every time a crowd laughs when I say something I mean, I feel connected, so much less alone.

I don't need to perform for hundreds of people to get that rush, either. I don't need to go into the most competitive clubs to test my mettle. Sometimes the best stand-up sets *are* the hard ones and the strange ones. The line between euphoria and depression is razor thin in stand-up, just like in real life.

There was a week where things were *not* going well at *The Chris Gethard Show.* We'd put up an episode that our network wasn't happy with. They wanted some major changes. Our next episode was fully written and ready to be produced; we had to throw the whole thing out and write an entire new episode that would go on live television in two days. Our producers were exhausted. Our writers spent fourteen-hour days cracking ideas in the writers' room. I was shell-shocked from the experience.

At the end of one of these days, I took the train from the office back to Jackson Heights. I climbed the subway steps slowly. I felt like I'd just finished up a fifteen-round boxing match. Physically, I was spent. Mentally, even more so. All I wanted to do was go home, collapse into bed, and hold my wife.

On the walk home, my stomach rumbled. I knew the coffee shop in my neighborhood would still be serving food. I could get a tuna melt, one of my ultimate comfort foods. I trudged up to the front window of Espresso 77, and as I reached the handle of the door I froze.

On the other side of the glass, a stand-up comedy show was happening.

I didn't even know my coffee shop had a stand-up night. By the looks of things, no one else really did either. There were nine people inside. One was the owner of the joint, sitting next to his friend. There was another guy sitting in the back of the place playing with his phone. Two teenagers sat with their arms around each other, clearly on a date and happy that comedy was taking place only to the degree that it allowed them to get handsy under the table. Everyone else was a comic. I knew just from sight alone. I know the ritual of my own kind, huddled in the back, laughing hard in an almost empty room to make each other feel like it was worth the trip out that night.

I opened the door and slipped into the back. The owner saw me, stood up, and walked over. He's known me for a while.

"Dude, do you want to perform?"

"I don't know," I said. "I don't want to step on anybody's toes. Why didn't you tell me you were doing stand-up? I would have put it in my schedule!"

"I didn't want to bother you yet," he said. "I figured I'd see if we could build a crowd. But you're here. I'm telling them to put you up."

He walked over to the host and whispered, gesturing toward me. She came by to shake my hand.

"I hope I'm not barging in," I told her.

"We had someone bail anyway," she said, disinterested. "Whatever."

I wrote down my name for her. After two more comics finished up, she sauntered to the mic and said, "Please welcome Chris Get Hard."

I'd already had an awful day. A brutal week. A stressful month. You may think performing for two fifteen-year-olds and the owner of the establishment was my nightmare. That night, it was my dream.

All I had to do was talk. To boil down my thoughts into punch lines that felt universal. The mic had a lot of feedback. The jokes didn't all work. The teens only laughed a handful of times. I don't blame them; they just wanted me to shut up so they could go fool around somewhere.

It was heaven. A couple of people laughing, and sometimes not. A sad little show no one knew about, where up-and-comers took trains to this far-flung corner of Queens because they heard there was a little stage time for them to cut their teeth with.

No one to yell at me. No teams stressed out waiting for me to lead a charge. No responsibility, no impact beyond the moment, no consequences beyond the ones that related to me and my craft and what I could learn about my jokes from telling them right here and right now.

Why this? Because it's the purest distillation of the dream I've held close to my vest since I was eight years old.

Why here? Because someone set up a mic in the corner and the owner said it was okay.

Why now? Because, oh God, I need to get a laugh. I need to do what I do. I need to remember that I don't do this for money, I don't do this for fame, I don't do this to make television network executives happy. I do this in the hopes that a couple of awkward fifteen-year-old kids might go, "Hey, that guy's pretty funny."

Because I've chipped away at my dream for two decades. I've seen it from every angle. I've taken it to some surprisingly high highs. But I know it's at its most real inside its low lows. It's easy to lose sight when the pressure's on. A sad show in a coffee shop is no pressure, nothing about it's gilded, and it *is my dream*.

And that is why I'm begging you; get out there and go for it, and fight tooth and nail to make your dreams come true. But please, as you do, take a deep breath and enjoy the ride. The joys you feel on the way to your dream might just be the dream themselves. Fail on the grandest stage you can reach, but don't forget—there's some version of this they can't take away from you. Find that, grab that, treasure that. It is the knowledge that will empower you beyond your silly dreams.

That's why I love stand-up more than anything. If I can get two people to laugh, no one can take it away. It's jokes. It's laughs. For me, it turns out it's the engine that powers everything else I've ever wanted to do.

Fight your fights and spend years on your quest, and be smart enough to notice your engine along the way. They can never take that away from you.

The travel that comes along with stand-up isn't all bad. I get to meet fans after shows, too, and despite the occasional well-meaning oversharer who doesn't know when to move on from a chat, meeting real people never gets old. In London I met a kid wearing a CHRIS GETHARD SHOW shirt featuring perhaps our dumbest all-time character, the Hintmaster. This kid told me he was the first person in England to order a T-shirt from us. I wrote him a handwritten letter expressing my thanks when he got it. He told me that the friend of his who got him into my show had died and he wanted to shake my hand on his deceased pal's behalf. I did so proudly. Out on the road I've met callers from *Beautiful/Anonymous*. These are people I've shared intense intimate moments with, and I get to look them in the eye. We share a secret. In person they're always nervous and I'm always awkward, but our person-to-person exchange always means so much. I've had hundreds of heart-to-heart talks with people who say *Career Suicide* helped them. It's even more meaningful to me when people say things like, "You helped me understand what my brother's going through." I've been through depression. I know how alone one can feel. To hear that family members understand, that friends step up—it makes me feel like maybe, just maybe, I've done my part to do some good in this world.

I can die happy if that's all I manage to do. A little bit of good. I'll take it.

And that's what I'm most grateful for at the end of the day: I don't live with an ounce of regret. I've made mistakes along the way. My career path was confusing and stressful, more often than not a consequence of my own missteps and insecurities. But I've laid it all on the line and, over time, proven that I can keep up. I've never been the most well-known comedian. I've never tasted real mainstream success. Hell, I've never been the funniest comedian. Not even close. But no one can deny I've been a comedian. The thing that once seemed like it wasn't even worth saying, wasn't even worth dreaming, is now my reality. It says so right on my tax returns. It's a living. And not just in the sense that it pays the bills. It's *living*.

I put it on the table. Somehow it worked out. My resilience served me well, probably better than my sense of humor. I am marginally talented at creating funny content, but I'm supremely talented at being my hardworking father's son. It's all going to be gone someday. *The Chris Gethard Show* will get canceled at some point. It may have even happened between the time I wrote these words and the time they were published. People will move on from *Beautiful/Anonymous*. A point will come when I'm not popular enough to pull off a road gig. The ticket sales will dry up. I'll stop getting booked.

I'll fade away. You'll forget me. I'll get a job. Probably not a desk job—I don't think I can handle that. I've always wanted to collect tickets on a train. I'd love that. Maybe someday I'll punch someone's ticket and they'll say, "Don't I know you?" I'll say, "Not anymore, but maybe you once did." They'll giggle uncomfortably, because that's an odd thing to say.

Maybe someday a far more successful comedian than I will get asked about how they got inspired to go for it. And maybe they'll say, "There was this kid. He made a public access show. It was him and his friends and it was pretty nuts. Almost no one knew about it. It came pretty close to going big but never got quite there. They did it their way. And they did it the right way."

Maybe somebody will crack the code I've never quite perfected and they'll thank me in their Emmy speech. I have mine all planned out. I don't think I'll ever get to say it. But I have a feeling one of the creative kids who rallied around my work might get there even though I couldn't.

That would make me happy.

I'll grow old and immobile. Hallie will take care of me. Even if I haven't gone onstage in decades, I'll make her laugh. That's really the only thing I owe the world: making Hallie laugh as a thank-you for all the times she murdered people to protect me in her dreams.

My wife and I have a plan to die at the same moment, of natural causes, while holding hands. I hope that's how it goes down, many years from now. If she goes first, I'm sure I'll head out a few weeks later. She's my heart, she keeps mine beating.

Life backed me into a corner and I had to push back. I hope you get a chance to do the same. And I hope because you've read this book you can skip fearing the fear. You can't avoid the fight and you can't cut the line, but maybe by knowing how I eventually realized the value of failure and fear you can laugh maniacally in the face of your own. Dive into it. The scarier the better. Choose to go off the deep end. Choose to play it unsafe. I want to hear what you have to say. I want to experience your art. I want to hear your songs, read your poems, buy the things you knit and sell on Etsy. I want to know you freed yourself from the fear, doubt, and shame of wondering what if.

So many people view me as an empathetic person, and it leads them to asking me: *How can I pull off my version of what you've done?*

In writing this book and thinking so hard about how to answer, I've come to realize that I don't think "how" is really the question any of you mean to ask. I think what you're really wondering is, "Can I?" You don't really care about methodology, you care about possibility. And "Can I?" is a much more difficult question to answer.

Because the answer is a simple but terrifying "I don't know." I don't know just as much as you don't know.

I don't think it really matters, though, because I don't think "Can I?" is the question you *mean* to be asking. There's the question you're asking: "How?" There's the question you're too nervous to ask: "Can I?" But the question you need to be asking is: "Should I?"

And to that, I can say without pause—the answer is yes.

You should. You always should.

Throw a brick through the window. Burn it down. Build it up. Fail spectacularly. And never, ever apologize.

I regret some of the things I've done, but I will *never* regret the things I haven't done. Because anything I've wanted to try, I've tried it. I failed often. I failed proudly. I lost well.

ACKNOWLEDGMENTS

This book would not exist without the support of many people. Hallie Bulleit, you are my greatest friend. To my parents, Ken and Sally, thank you for letting me be who I am. And to my family on all sides, especially Gregg and Ilana Gethard. Ethan Bassoff, Isaac Dunham, and Brian Stern, thank you for overseeing all the icky stuff I'm not built to handle. A massive thanks to Justin Linville for supporting the infrastructure of my life; please remember me when you own half of Los Angeles and hold all of our fates in your hands. Thank you to Miles Doyle for taking a chance on me—I sincerely hope you don't regret it. Thanks to my *TCGS* family, especially my creative rock, J.D. Amato. Thanks to Earwolf, Jared O'Connell, Harry Nelson, and all the listeners of *Beautiful/Anonymous* who changed my life. Thanks to Mike Berkowitz and Marcus Levy for getting me out on the road where I can experience real truth. Thanks to the many role models I've had in the comedy world, who have supported me oftentimes well before I deserved it: Mike Birbiglia, Judd Apatow, Will Ferrell, Adam McKay, Owen Burke, and the Upright Citizens Brigade come to mind. Thanks to Mark Moran and Mark Sceurman for creating something cool and letting me see how the gears turn. Thanks to the hundreds of artists

in my life who continuously inspire me, including but not limited to
Antonio Campos, Jeff Rosenstock, Mal Blum, Tom Scharpling, Don
Fanelli, Mike Campbell, Laura Stevenson, and Jo Firestone. Thanks
to the Comedy Cellar for challenging me to be my best. Thanks to
the life-changing institution that is the Manhattan Neighborhood
Network. Protect public access, support public access, consume public access. The corporations want to take it away and you must not let
them. Last but not least, thanks to the great state of New Jersey. I'll be
back someday.